# Alfred's Basic Guitar Chor

M000166593

## TABLE OF CONTENTS

## CHORDS

*Enharmonic Equivalents*

| | A♭ G# | A | B♭ A# | B C♭ | C | D♭ C# | D | E♭ D# | E | F | F# G♭ | G |
|---|---|---|---|---|---|---|---|---|---|---|---|---|
| Major | 10 | 16 | 22 | 28 | 34 | 40 | 46 | 52 | 58 | 64 | 70 | 76 |
| Major Suspended Fourth | 10 | 16 | 22 | 28 | 34 | 40 | 46 | 52 | 58 | 64 | 70 | 76 |
| Flat Fifth | 10 | 16 | 22 | 28 | 34 | 40 | 46 | 52 | 58 | 64 | 70 | 76 |
| Major Add Ninth | 10 | 16 | 22 | 28 | 34 | 40 | 46 | 52 | 58 | 64 | 70 | 76 |
| Fifth | 10 | 16 | 22 | 28 | 34 | 40 | 46 | 52 | 58 | 64 | 70 | 76 |
| Minor | 10 | 16 | 22 | 28 | 34 | 40 | 46 | 52 | 58 | 64 | 70 | 76 |
| Augmented | 11 | 17 | 23 | 29 | 35 | 41 | 47 | 53 | 59 | 65 | 71 | 77 |
| Diminished | 11 | 17 | 23 | 29 | 35 | 41 | 47 | 53 | 59 | 65 | 71 | 77 |
| Major Sixth | 11 | 17 | 23 | 29 | 35 | 41 | 47 | 53 | 59 | 65 | 71 | 77 |
| Sixth Add Ninth | 11 | 17 | 23 | 29 | 35 | 41 | 47 | 53 | 59 | 65 | 71 | 77 |
| Minor Sixth Add Ninth | 11 | 17 | 23 | 29 | 35 | 41 | 47 | 53 | 59 | 65 | 71 | 77 |
| Minor Sixth | 11 | 17 | 23 | 29 | 35 | 41 | 47 | 53 | 59 | 65 | 71 | 77 |
| Seventh | 12 | 18 | 24 | 30 | 36 | 42 | 48 | 54 | 60 | 66 | 72 | 78 |
| Seventh Suspended Fourth | 12 | 18 | 24 | 30 | 36 | 42 | 48 | 54 | 60 | 66 | 72 | 78 |
| Minor Seventh | 12 | 18 | 24 | 30 | 36 | 42 | 48 | 54 | 60 | 66 | 72 | 78 |
| Minor Seventh Flat Fifth | 12 | 18 | 24 | 30 | 36 | 42 | 48 | 54 | 60 | 66 | 72 | 78 |
| Seventh Augmented Fifth | 12 | 18 | 24 | 30 | 36 | 42 | 48 | 54 | 60 | 66 | 72 | 78 |
| Seventh Flat Fifth | 12 | 18 | 24 | 30 | 36 | 42 | 48 | 54 | 60 | 66 | 72 | 78 |
| Major Seventh | 13 | 19 | 25 | 31 | 37 | 43 | 49 | 55 | 61 | 67 | 73 | 79 |
| Major Seventh Flat Fifth | 13 | 19 | 25 | 31 | 37 | 43 | 49 | 55 | 61 | 67 | 73 | 79 |
| Minor Major Seventh | 13 | 19 | 25 | 31 | 37 | 43 | 49 | 55 | 61 | 67 | 73 | 79 |
| Seventh Flat Ninth | 13 | 19 | 25 | 31 | 37 | 43 | 49 | 55 | 61 | 67 | 73 | 79 |
| Seventh Augmented Ninth | 13 | 19 | 25 | 31 | 37 | 43 | 49 | 55 | 61 | 67 | 73 | 79 |
| Seventh Flat Ninth Augmented Fifth | 13 | 19 | 25 | 31 | 37 | 43 | 49 | 55 | 61 | 67 | 73 | 79 |
| Minor Ninth | 14 | 20 | 26 | 32 | 38 | 44 | 50 | 56 | 62 | 68 | 74 | 80 |
| Ninth | 14 | 20 | 26 | 32 | 38 | 44 | 50 | 56 | 62 | 68 | 74 | 80 |
| Ninth Augmented Fifth | 14 | 20 | 26 | 32 | 38 | 44 | 50 | 56 | 62 | 68 | 74 | 80 |
| Ninth Flat Fifth | 14 | 20 | 26 | 32 | 38 | 44 | 50 | 56 | 62 | 68 | 74 | 80 |
| Major Ninth | 14 | 20 | 26 | 32 | 38 | 44 | 50 | 56 | 62 | 68 | 74 | 80 |
| Ninth Augmented Eleventh | 14 | 20 | 26 | 32 | 38 | 44 | 50 | 56 | 62 | 68 | 74 | 80 |
| Minor Ninth Major Seventh | 15 | 21 | 27 | 33 | 39 | 45 | 51 | 57 | 63 | 69 | 75 | 81 |
| Eleventh | 15 | 21 | 27 | 33 | 39 | 45 | 51 | 57 | 63 | 69 | 75 | 81 |
| Minor Eleventh | 15 | 21 | 27 | 33 | 39 | 45 | 51 | 57 | 63 | 69 | 75 | 81 |
| Thirteenth | 15 | 21 | 27 | 33 | 39 | 45 | 51 | 57 | 63 | 69 | 75 | 81 |
| Thirteenth Flat Ninth | 15 | 21 | 27 | 33 | 39 | 45 | 51 | 57 | 63 | 69 | 75 | 81 |
| Thirteenth Flat Ninth Flat Fifth | 15 | 21 | 27 | 33 | 39 | 45 | 51 | 57 | 63 | 69 | 75 | 81 |

Guitar photo courtesy of
the Martin Guitar Company.

Alfred

# CHORD THEORY

Play any note on the guitar, then play a note one fret above it. The distance between these two notes is a *half step*. Play another note followed by a note two frets above it. The distance between these two notes is a *whole step* (two half steps). The distance between any two notes is referred to as an *interval*.

In the example of the C major scale below, the letter names are shown above the notes and the *scale degrees* (numbers) of the notes are written below. Notice that C is the first degree of the scale, D is the second, etc.

The name of an interval is determined by counting the number of scale degrees from one note to the next. For example: An interval of a 3rd, starting on C, would be determined by counting up three scale degrees, or C-D-E (1-2-3). C to E is a 3rd. An interval of a 4th, starting on C, would be determined by counting up four scale degrees, or C-D-E-F (1-2-3-4). C to F is a 4th.

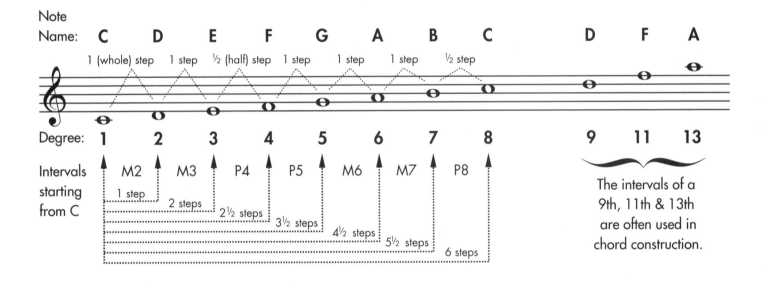

Intervals are not only labeled by the distance between scale degrees, but by the *quality* of the interval. An interval's quality is determined by counting the number of whole steps and half steps between the two notes of an interval. For example: C to E is a 3rd. C to E is also a major third because there are 2 whole steps between C and E. Likewise, C to E♭ is a 3rd. C to E♭ is also a minor third because there are 1½ steps between C and E♭. There are five qualities used to describe intervals: *major, minor, perfect, diminished and augmented*.

**M = Major     m = Minor     P = Perfect     ° = Diminished (dim)     + = Augmented (aug)**

Particular intervals are associated with certain qualities:

| | | |
|---|---|---|
| 2nds, 9ths | = | Major, Minor & Augmented |
| 3rds, 6ths, 13ths | = | Major, Minor, Augmented & Diminished |
| 4ths, 5ths, 11ths | = | Perfect, Augmented & Diminished |
| 7ths | = | Major, Minor & Diminished |

# Intervals

When a *major* interval is made **smaller** by a half step it becomes a *minor* interval.

When a *minor* interval is made **larger** by a half step it becomes a *major* interval.

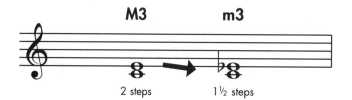

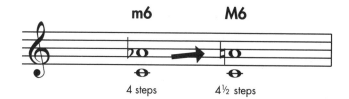

When a *minor* or *perfect* interval is made **smaller** by a half step it becomes a *diminished* interval.

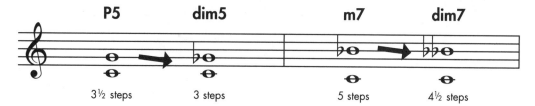

When a *major* or *perfect* interval is made **larger** by a half step it becomes an *augmented* interval.

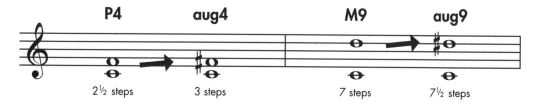

Below is a Table of Intervals starting on the note C. Notice that some intervals are labeled *enharmonic*, which means that they are written differently but sound the same (see **aug2** & **m3**).

## TABLE OF INTERVALS

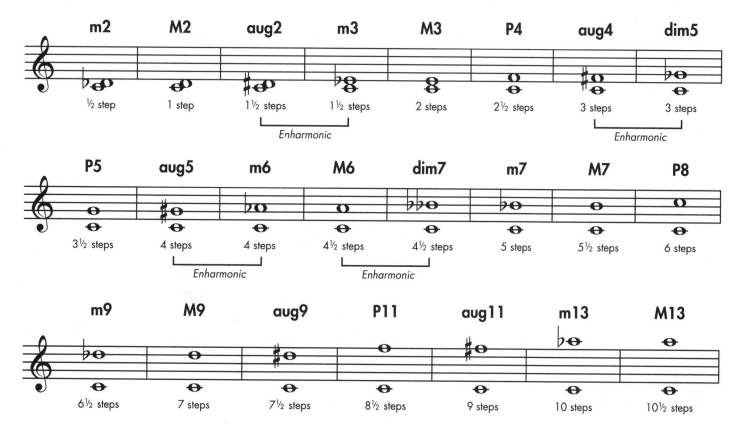

# CHORD THEORY

Two or more notes played together is called a *chord*. Most commonly, a chord will consist of three or more notes. A three-note chord is called a *triad*. The *root* of a triad (or any other chord) is the note from which a chord is constructed. The relationship of the intervals from the root to the other notes of a chord determines the *chord type*. Triads are most frequently identified by four chord types: *major, minor, diminished and augmented*.

All chord types can be identified by the intervals used to create the chord. For example; the C major triad is built beginning with C as the root, adding a major 3rd (E) and adding a perfect 5th (G). All major triads contain a root, M3 and P5.

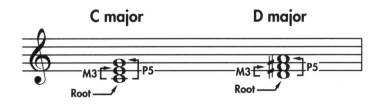

Minor triads contain a root, minor 3rd and perfect 5th. (An easier way to build a minor triad is to simply lower the 3rd of a major triad.) All minor triads contain a root, m3 and P5.

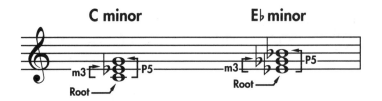

Diminished triads contain a root, minor 3rd and diminished 5th. If the perfect 5th of a minor triad is made smaller by a half step (to become a diminished 5th), the result is a diminished triad. All diminished triads contain a root, m3 and dim5.

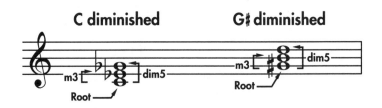

Augmented triads contain a root, major 3rd and augmented 5th. If the perfect 5th of a major triad is made larger by a half step (to become an augmented 5th), the result is an augmented triad. All augmented triads contain a root, M3 and aug5.

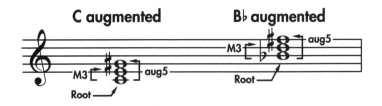

An important concept to remember about chords is that the bottom note of a chord will not always be the root. If the root of a triad, for instance, is moved above the 5th so that the 3rd is the bottom note of the chord, it is said to be in the *first inversion*. If the root and 3rd are moved above the 5th, the chord is in the *second inversion*. The number of inversions that a chord can have is related to the number of notes in the chord—a three-note chord can have two inversions, a four-note chord can have three inversions, etc.

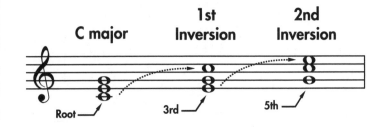

# Building Chords

By using the four chord types as basic building blocks, it is possible to create a variety of chords by adding 6ths, 7ths, 9ths, 11ths, etc.  The following are examples of some of the many variations:

\* The *Suspended Fourth* chord does not contain a third.  An assumption is made that the 4th degree of the chord will harmonically be inclined to *resolve* to the 3rd degree.  In other words, the 4th is *suspended* until it moves to the 3rd.

Thus far, the examples provided to illustrate intervals and chord construction have been based on C. Until familiarity with chords is achieved, the C chord examples on page 5 can serve as a reference guide when building chords based on other notes. For instance, locate C7(♭9) on page 5. To construct a G7(♭9) chord first determine what intervals are contained in C7(♭9) then follow the steps outlined below.

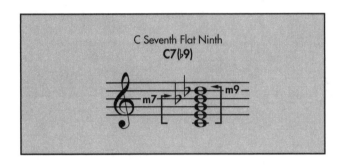

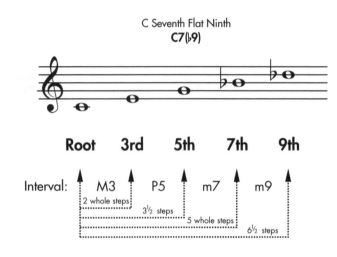

- Determine the *root* of the chord. A chord is always named for its root—in this instance, G is the root of G7(♭9).

- Count *letter names* up from the *letter name of the root* (G), as was done when building intervals on page 2, to determine the intervals of the chord. Therefore, counting 3 letter names up from G to B (G-A-B, 1-2-3) is a third, G to D (G-A-B-C-D) is a fifth, G to F is a seventh and G to A is a ninth.

- Determine the *quality* of the intervals by counting whole steps and half steps up from the root; G to B is a major 3rd (2 whole steps), G to D (3½ steps) is a perfect 5th, G to F (5 whole steps) is a minor seventh and G to A♭ (6½ steps) is a minor ninth.

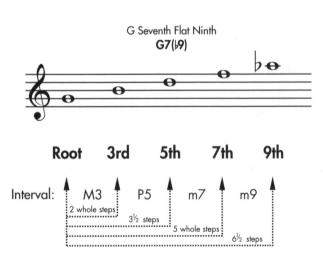

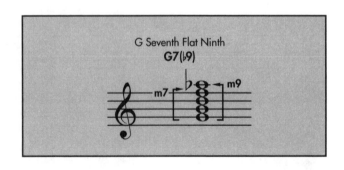

Follow this general guideline for determining the notes of any chord. As interval and chord construction become more familiar to the beginning guitarist, it will become possible to create original fingerings on the guitar. Experimentation is suggested.

## Circle of Fifths

The function of **Alfred's Basic Guitar Chord Dictionary** is to provide access to fingerings of thousands of guitar chords as well as introducing the fundamentals of chord construction. As the beginning guitarist becomes accomplished in the recognition and construction of intervals and chords, the next natural step is to seek an understanding of the *function* of these chords within *keys* or *chord progressions*. Although it is not fundamental to playing chord changes, further study in harmony and chord progressions can only enrich the musical experience of the advancing guitarist and is therefore highly recommended.

**Alfred's Basic Guitar Chord Dictionary** is organized to provide the fingerings of chords in all keys. The *Circle of Fifths* below will help to clarify which chords are enharmonic equivalents (notice that *chords* can be written enharmonically as well as *notes*—see page 3). The Circle of Fifths also serves as a quick reference guide to the relationship of the keys and how key signatures can be figured out in a logical manner. Clockwise movement (up a P5) provides all of the sharp keys by adding one sharp to the key signature progressively. Counter-clockwise (down a P5) provides the flat keys by adding one flat similarly.

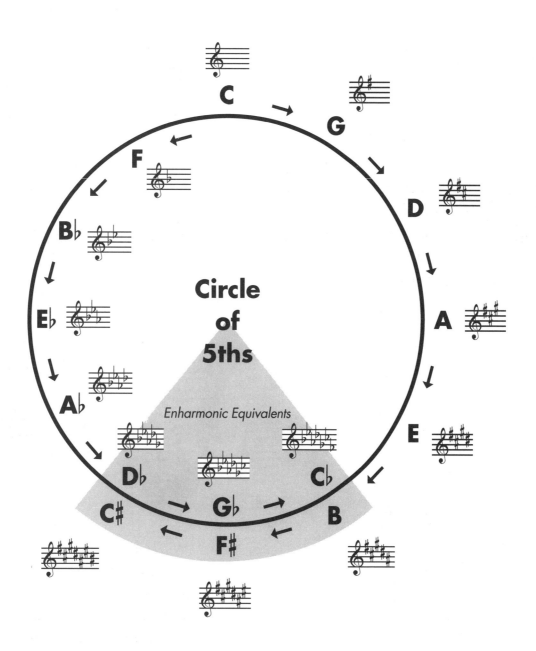

# READING CHORDS

# Chord Symbol Variations

Chord symbols are a form of musical shorthand providing the guitarist with as much information about a chord as quickly as possible. The intent of using chord symbols is to convey enough information to recognize the chord yet not so much as to confuse the meaning of the symbol. Since chord symbols are not universally standardized, they are often written in many different ways—some are understandable, others are confusing. To illustrate this point, below is a listing of *some* of the ways copyists, composers and arrangers have created variations on the more common chord symbols:

| C | Csus | C($\flat$5) | C(add9) | C5 | Cm |
|---|---|---|---|---|---|
| C major | Csus4 | C-5 | C(9) | C(no3) | Cmin |
| Cmaj | C(addF) | C(5-) | C(add2) | C(omit3) | Cmi |
| CM | C4 | C($\sharp$4) | C(+9) | | C- |
| | | | C(+D) | | |

| C+ | C° | C6 | C6/9 | Cm6/9 | Cm6 |
|---|---|---|---|---|---|
| C+5 | Cdim | Cmaj6 | C6(add9) | C-6/9 | C-6 |
| Caug | Cdim7 | C(addA) | C6(addD) | Cm6(+9) | Cm(addA) |
| Caug5 | C7dim | C(A) | C9(no7) | Cm6(add9) | Cm(+6) |
| C($\sharp$5) | | | C9/6 | Cm6(+D) | |

| C7 | C7sus | Cm7 | Cm7($\flat$5) | C7+ | C7($\flat$5) |
|---|---|---|---|---|---|
| C(addB$\flat$) | C7sus4 | Cmi7 | Cmi7-5 | C7+5 | C7-5 |
| C$\overline{7}$ | Csus7 | Cmin7 | C-7(5-) | C7aug | C7(5-) |
| C(-7) | C7(+4) | C-7 | C$\varnothing$ | C7aug5 | C$\overline{7}$-5 |
| C(+7) | | C7mi | C $\frac{1}{2}$dim | C7($\sharp$5) | C7($\sharp$4) |

| Cmaj7 | Cmaj7($\flat$5) | Cm(maj7) | C7($\flat$9) | C7($\sharp$9) | C7+($\flat$9) |
|---|---|---|---|---|---|
| Cma7 | Cmaj7(-5) | C-maj7 | C7(-9) | C7(+9) | Caug7-9 |
| C$\overline{7}$ | C$\overline{7}$(-5) | C-$\overline{7}$ | C9$\flat$ | C9$\sharp$ | C+7($\flat$9) |
| C$\triangle$ | C$\triangle$($\flat$5) | Cmi$\overline{7}$ | C9- | C9+ | C+9$\flat$ |
| C$\triangle$7 | | | | | C7+(-9) |

| Cm9 | C9 | C9+ | C9($\flat$5) | Cmaj9 | C9($\sharp$11) |
|---|---|---|---|---|---|
| Cm7(9) | C$\overline{7}^{9}$ | C9(+5) | C9(-5) | C$\overline{7}$(9) | C9(+11) |
| Cm7(+9) | C7add9 | Caug9 | C7$^{9}_{-5}$ | C$\overline{7}$(+9) | C($\sharp$11) |
| C-9 | C7(addD) | C($\sharp$9$\sharp$5) | C9(5$\flat$) | C9(maj7) | C11+ |
| Cmi7(9+) | C7(+9) | C+9 | | C$\overline{9}$ | C11$\sharp$ |

| Cm9(maj7) | C11 | Cm11 | C13 | C13($\flat$9) | C13($^{\flat 9}_{\flat 5}$) |
|---|---|---|---|---|---|
| C-9($\sharp$7) | C9(11) | C-11 | C9addA | C13(-9) | C13(-9-5) |
| C(-9)$\overline{7}$ | C9addF | Cm($\flat$11) | C9(6) | C$\flat^{13}_{9}$ | C($\flat$9$\flat$5)addA |
| Cmi9($\sharp$7) | C9+11 | Cmi7$^{11}_{9}$ | C7addA | C($\flat$9)addA | |
| | C7$^{9}_{11}$ | C-7($^{9}_{11}$) | C7+A | | |

# Chord Frames

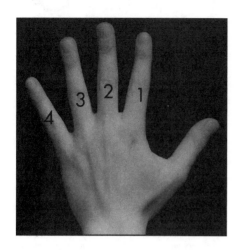

Guitar chord frames are diagrams that contain all the information necessary to play a particular chord. The fingerings, note names and position of the chord on the neck are all provided on the chord frame (see below). The photograph at left shows which finger number corresponds to which finger.

Choose chord positions that require the least motion from one chord to the next; select fingerings that are in approximately the same location on the guitar neck. This will provide smoother and more comfortable transitions between chords in a progression.

The following examples explain the various chord frame symbols.

**The number of the fret on which the fingers are positioned**

**Vertical lines represent the strings**

**Horizontal lines represent the frets**

1
2
3
4
5

(E  A  D  G  B  E)

**The notes of the open strings**

**An X indicates that the string is unplayed or muted**

**Open (unfingered) strings**

X  O        O

1
2    ②③④
3
4
5

A  E  A  C#  E

**Circles indicate on which fret and which string the finger is placed— the number indicates which finger is used**

**Slurs indicate that the finger is placed flat, covering the marked notes**

X

12    ❶        ❶
13
14    ❸❸❸
15
16

A  E  A  C#  E

**Resulting note names**

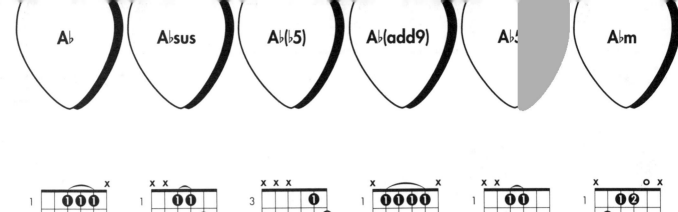

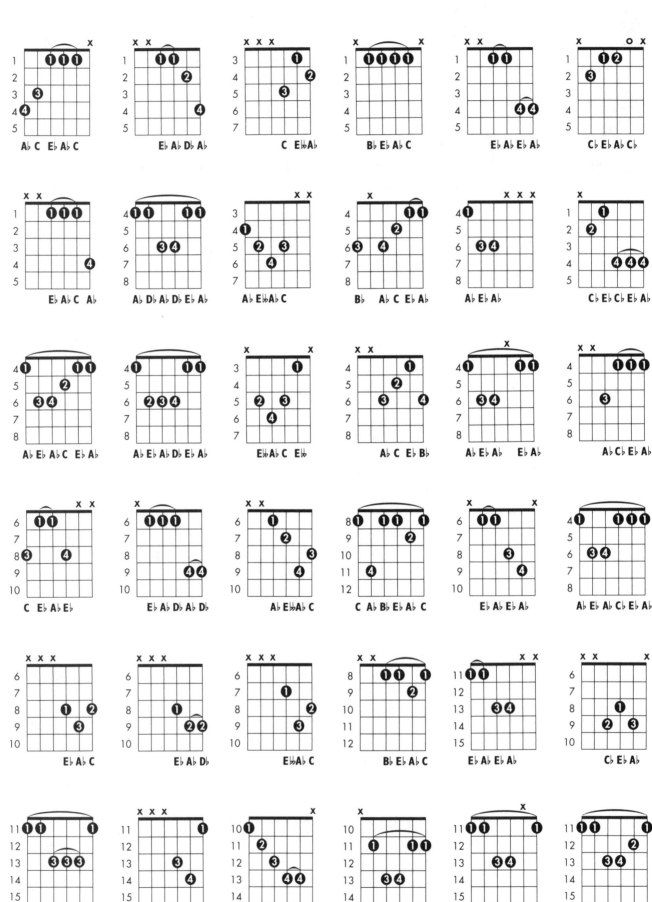

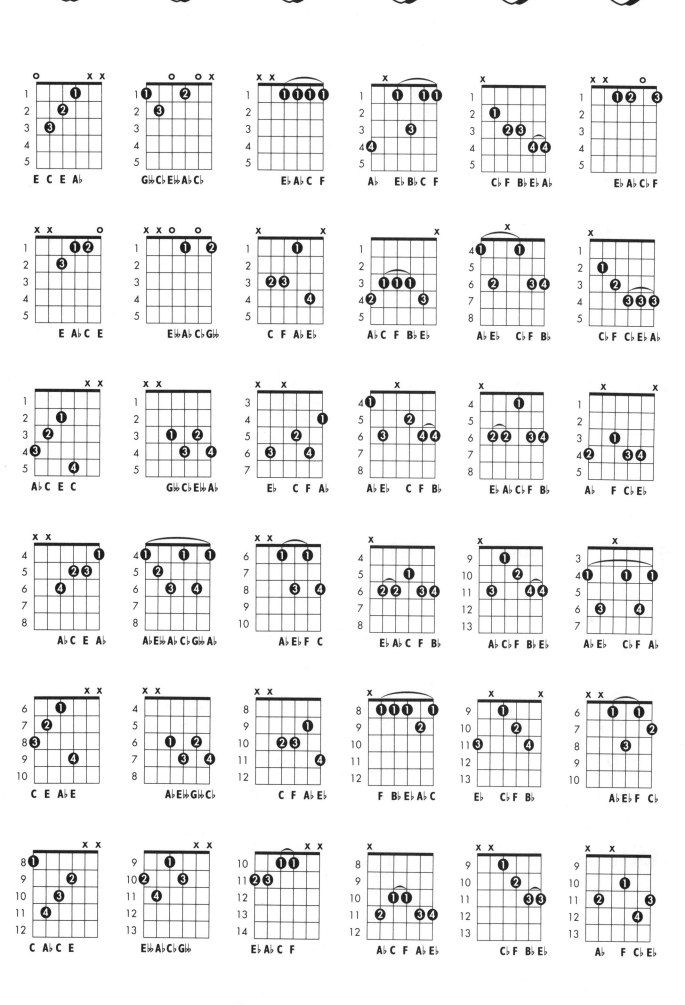

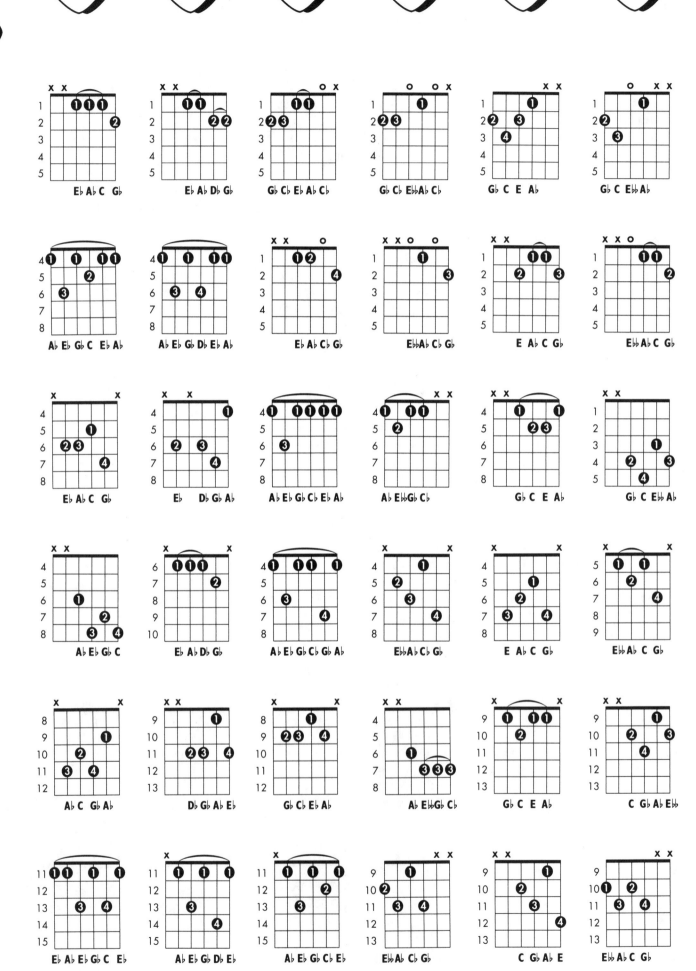

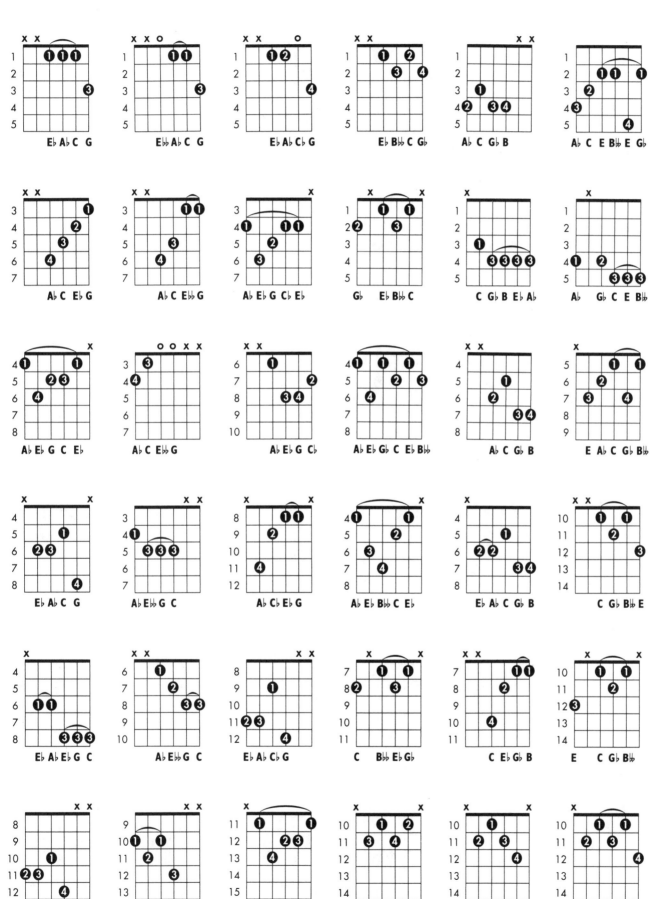

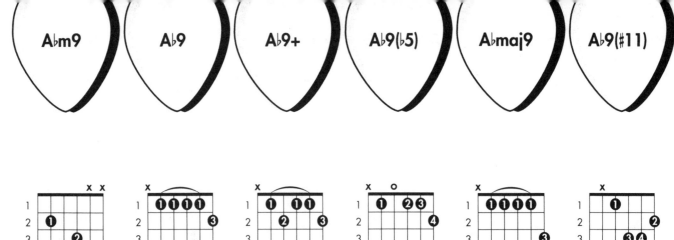

Ab

Abm9 | Ab9 | Ab9+ | Ab9(b5) | Abmaj9 | Ab9(#11)

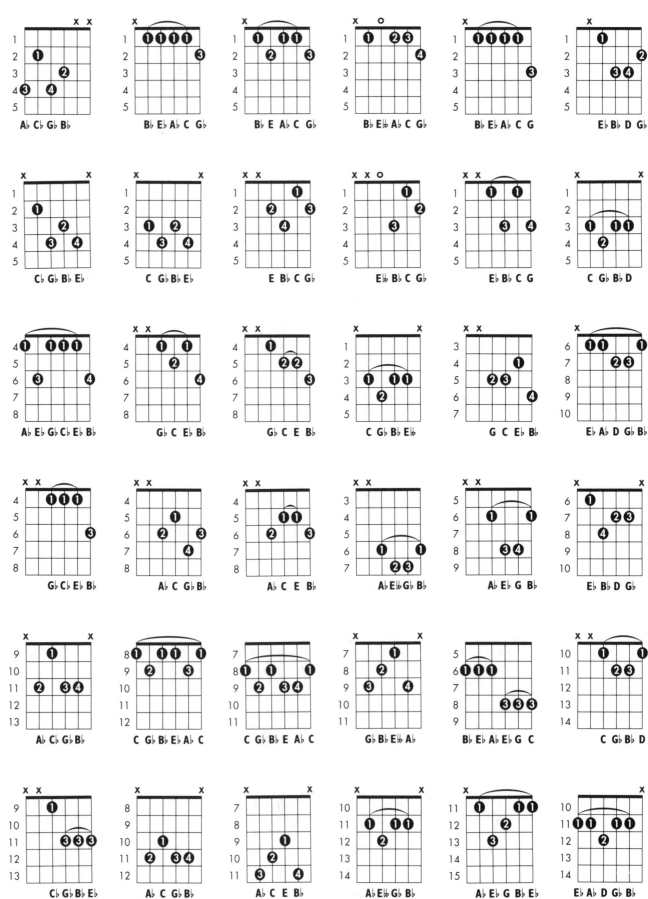

Row 1:
Ab Cb Gb Bb | Bb Eb Ab C Gb | Bb E Ab C Gb | Bb Eb Ab C Gb | Bb Eb Ab C G | Eb Bb D Gb

Row 2:
Cb Gb Bb Eb | C Gb Bb Eb | E Bb C Gb | Eb Bb C Gb | Eb Bb C G | C Gb Bb D

Row 3:
Ab Eb Gb Cb Eb Bb | Gb C Eb Bb | Gb C E Bb | C Gb Bb Eb | G C Eb Bb | Eb Ab D Gb Bb

Row 4:
Gb Cb Eb Bb | Ab C Gb Bb | Ab C E Bb | Ab Eb Gb Bb | Ab Eb G Bb | Eb Bb D Gb

Row 5:
Ab Cb Gb Bb | C Gb Bb Eb Ab C | C Gb Bb E Ab C | Gb Bb Eb Ab | Bb Eb Ab Eb G C | C Gb Bb D

Row 6:
Cb Gb Bb Eb | Ab C Gb Bb | Ab C E Bb | Ab Eb Gb Bb | Ab Eb G Bb Eb | Eb Ab D Gb Bb

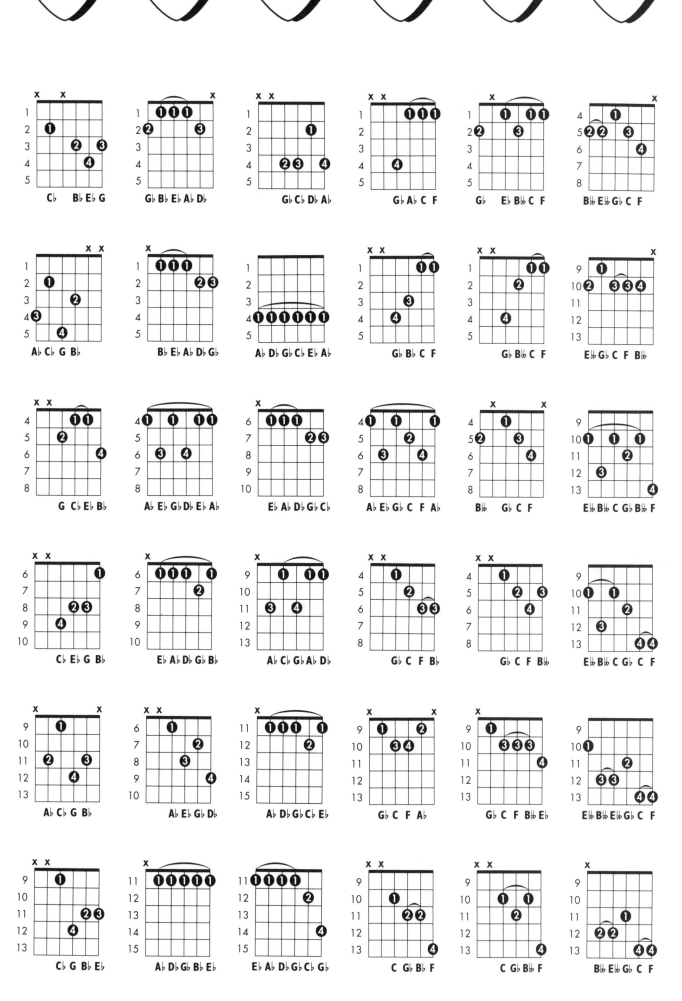

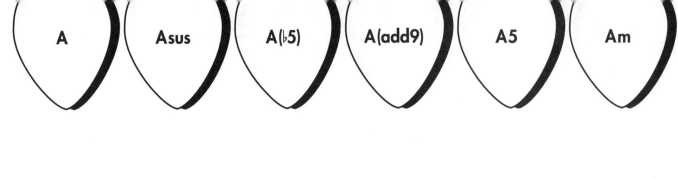

A

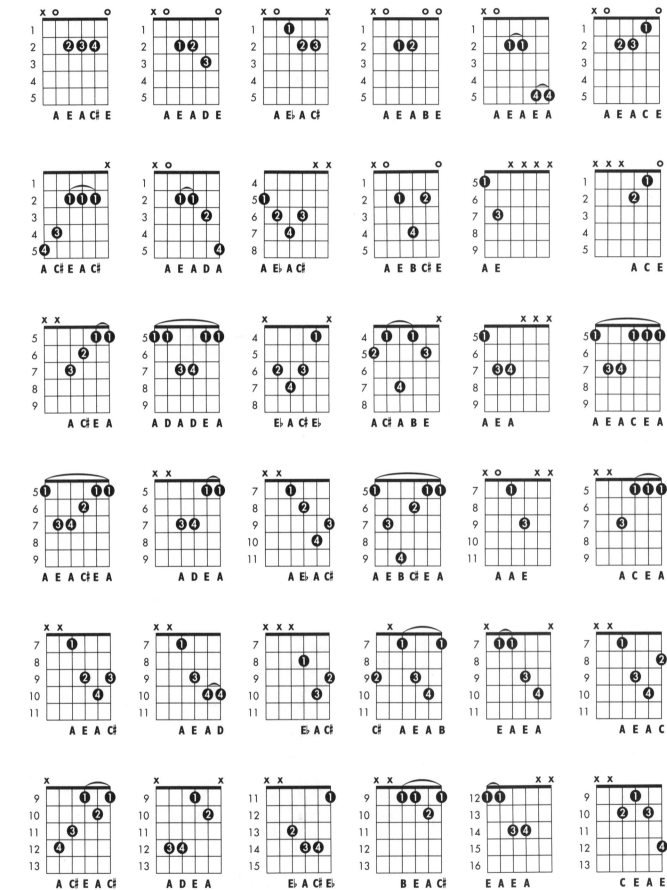

| A+ | A° | A6 | A6/9 | Am6/9 | Am6 |
|---|---|---|---|---|---|

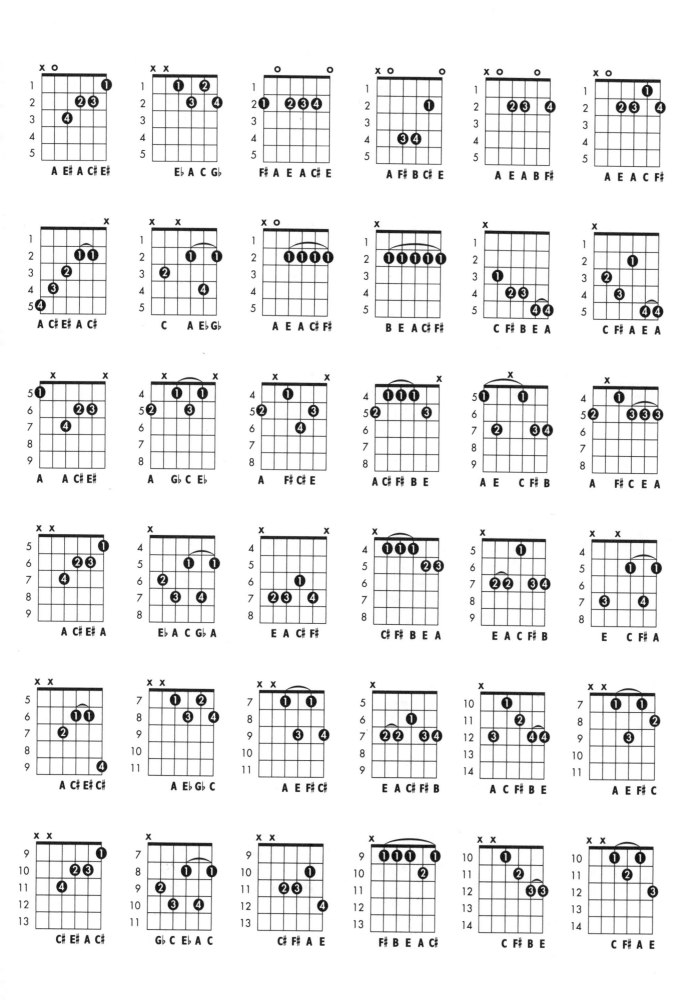

**A**

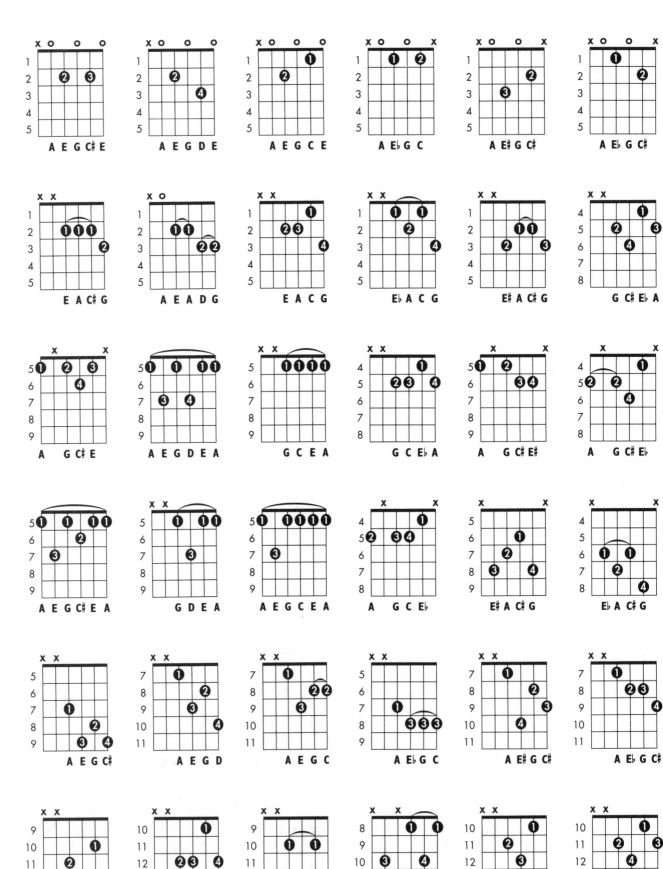

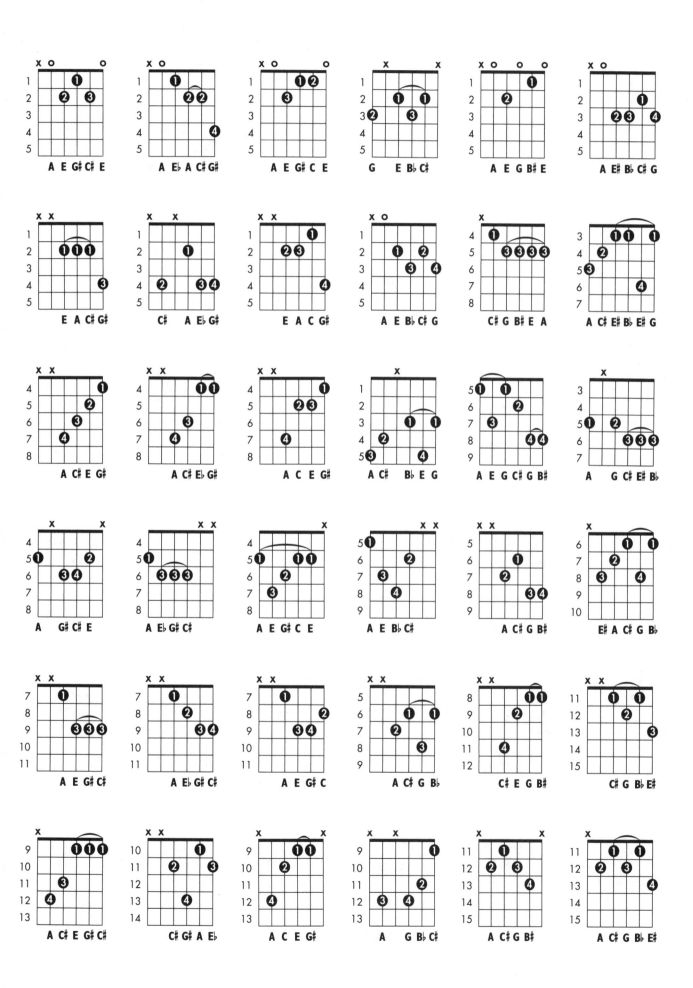

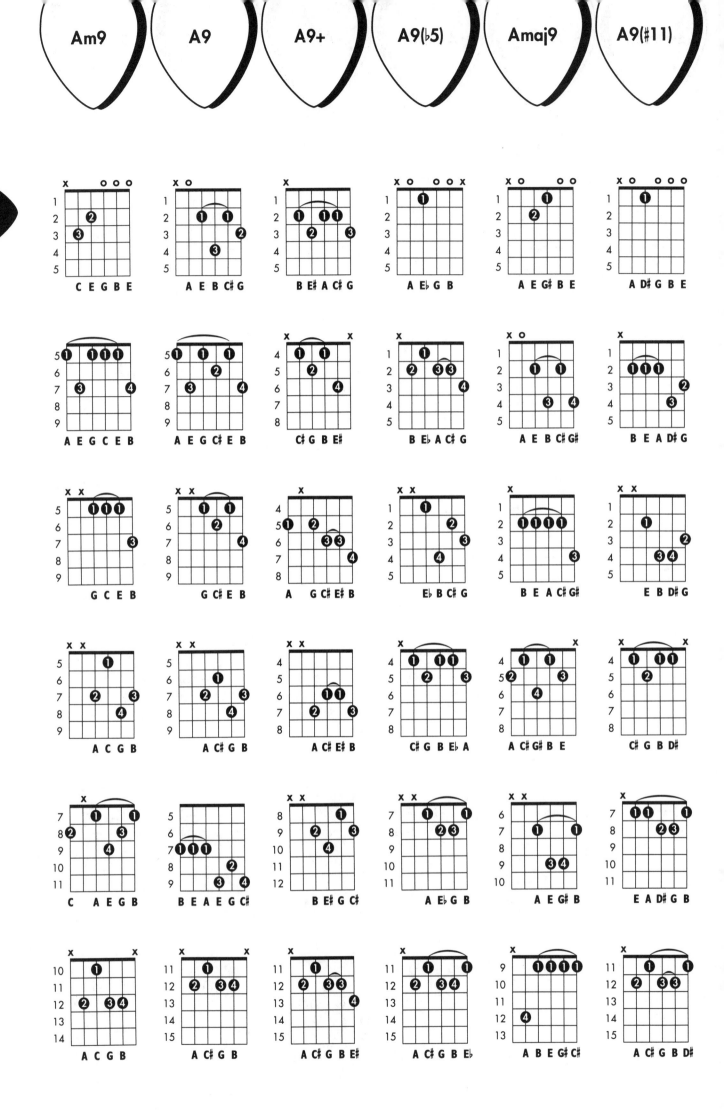

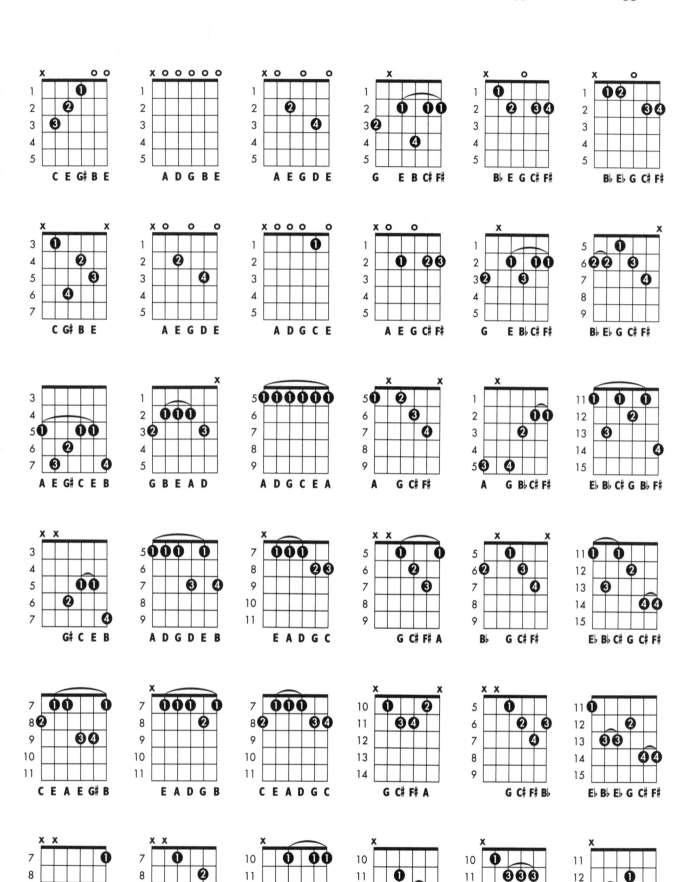

**B♭**   **B♭sus**   **B♭(♭5)**   **B♭(add9)**   **B♭5**   **B♭m**

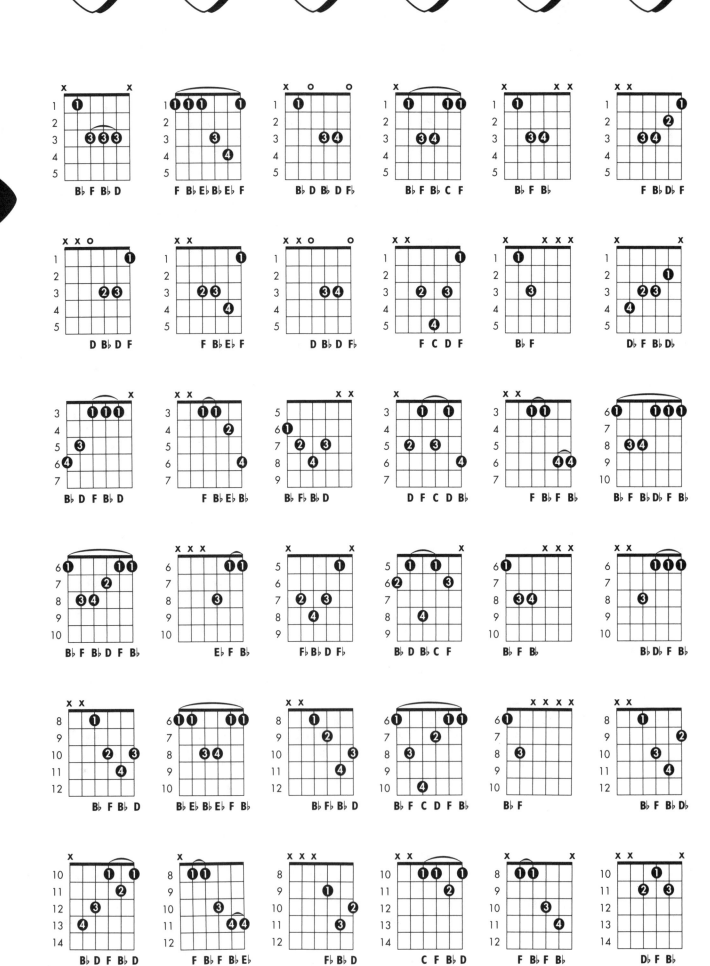

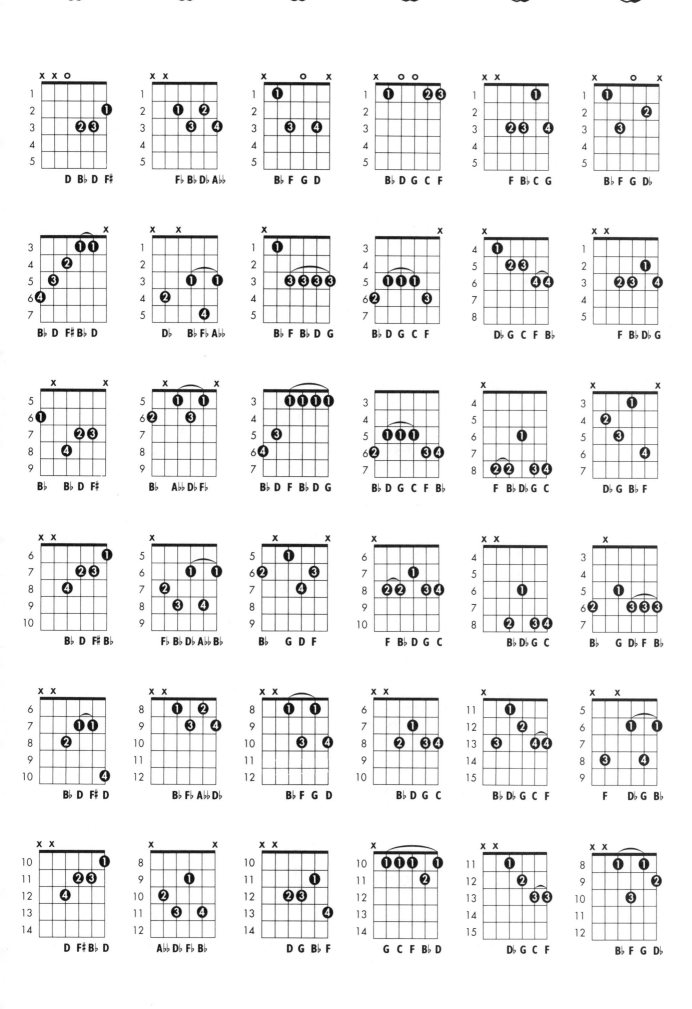

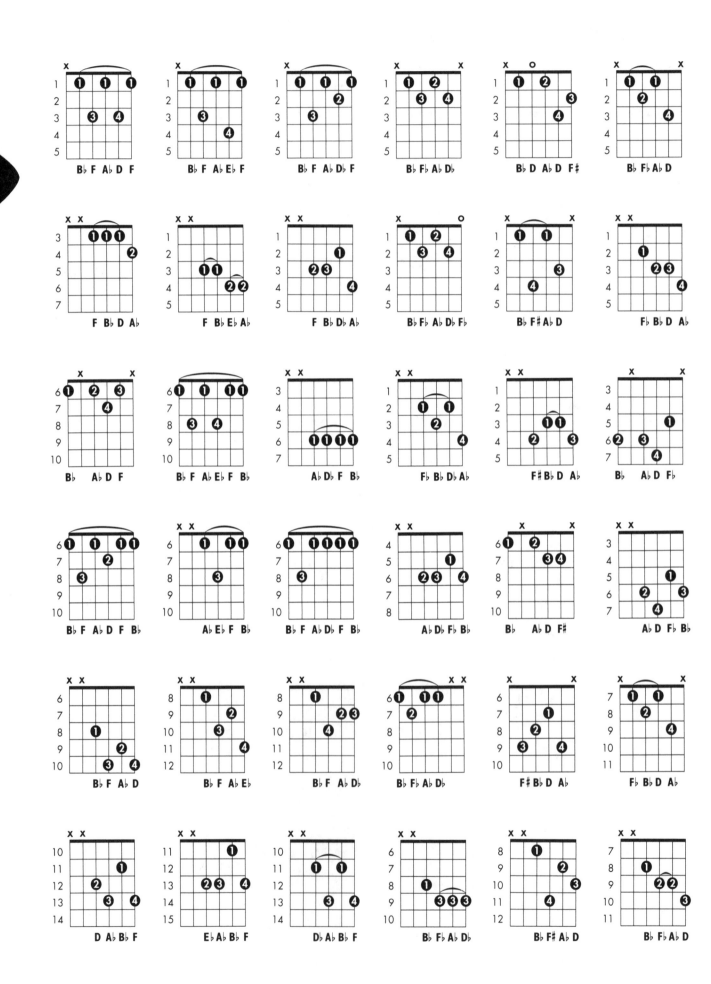

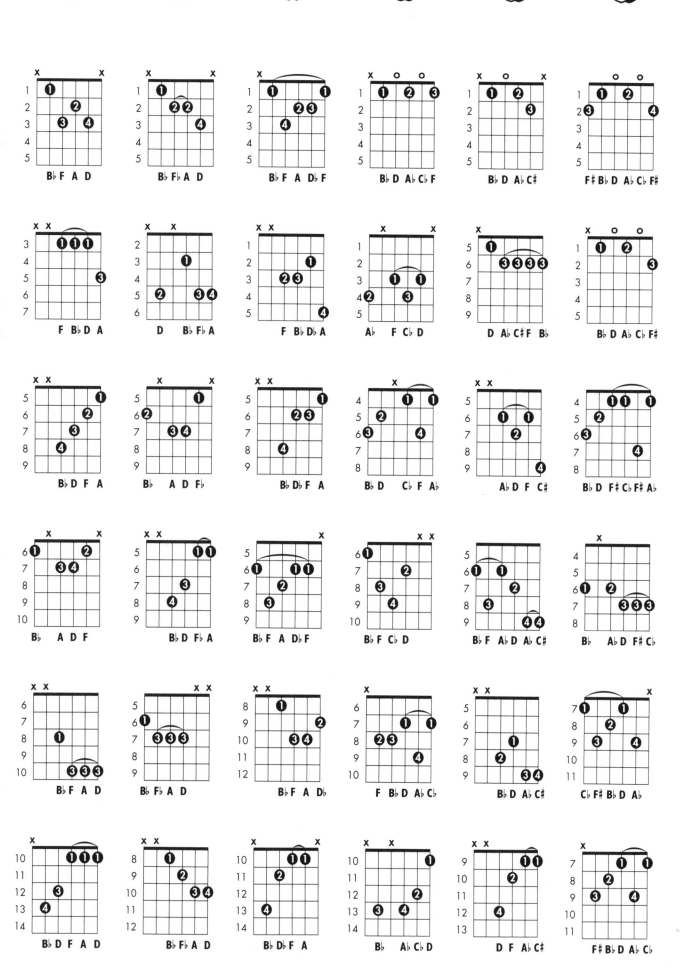

B♭maj7    B♭maj7(♭5)    B♭m(maj7)    B♭7(♭9)    B♭7(#9)    B♭7+(♭9)

B♭

26

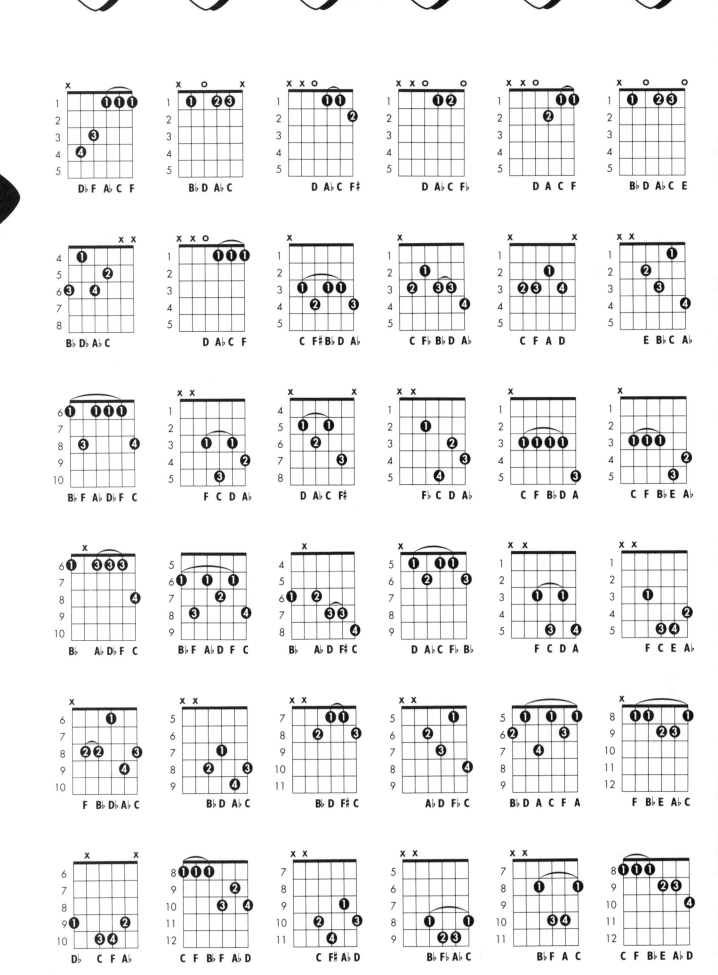

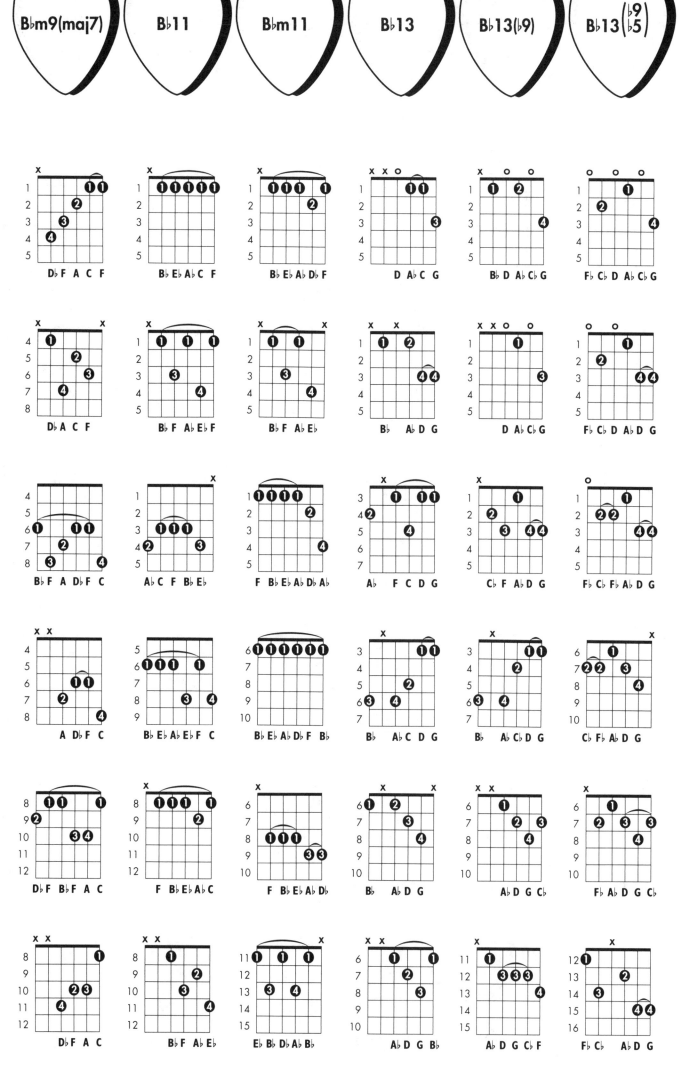

**B**  **Bsus**  **B(♭5)**  **B(add9)**  **B5**  **Bm**

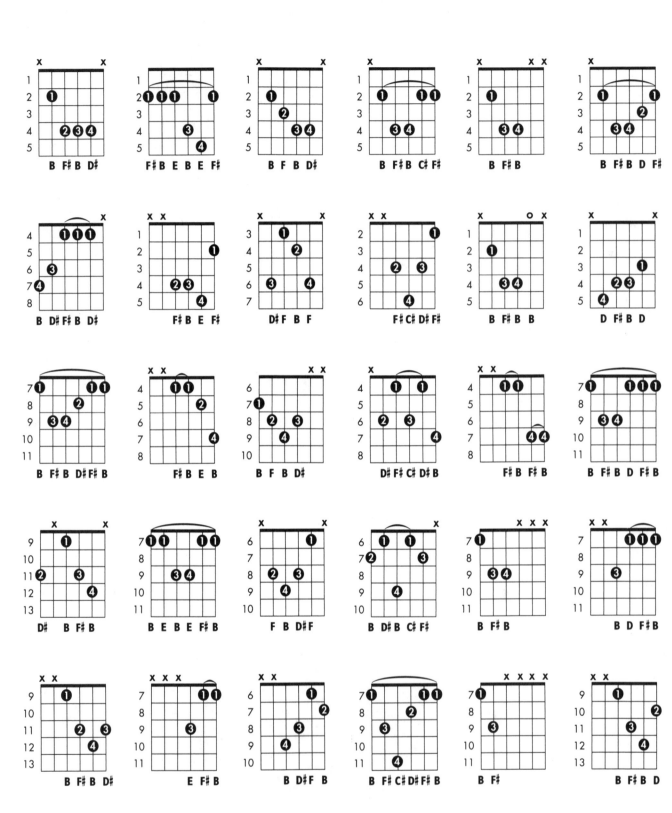

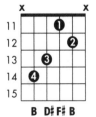
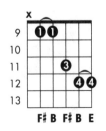
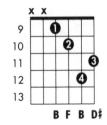
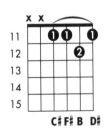
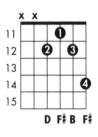

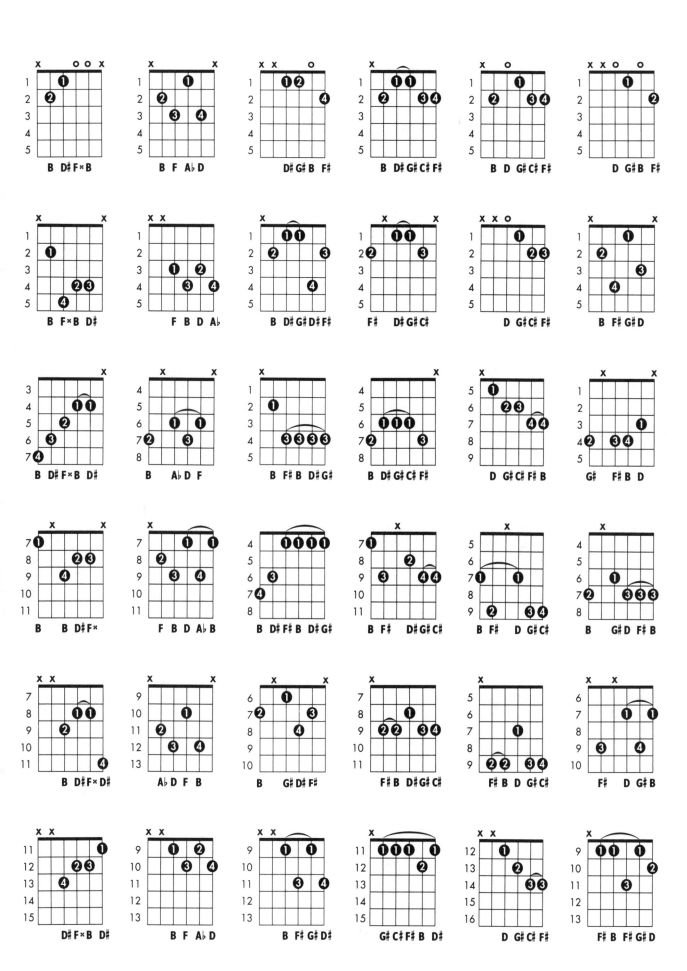

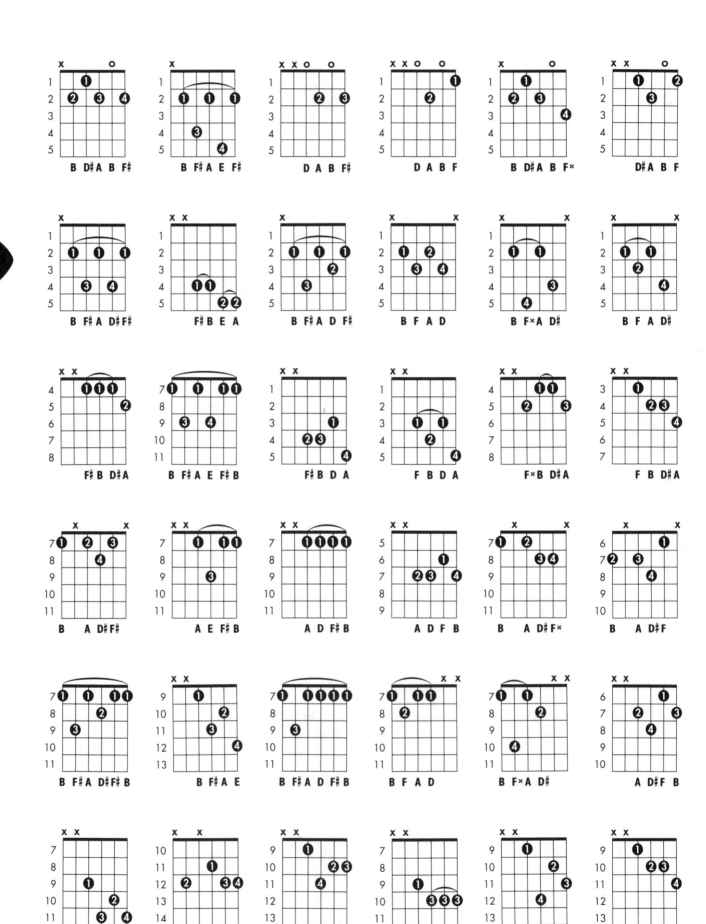

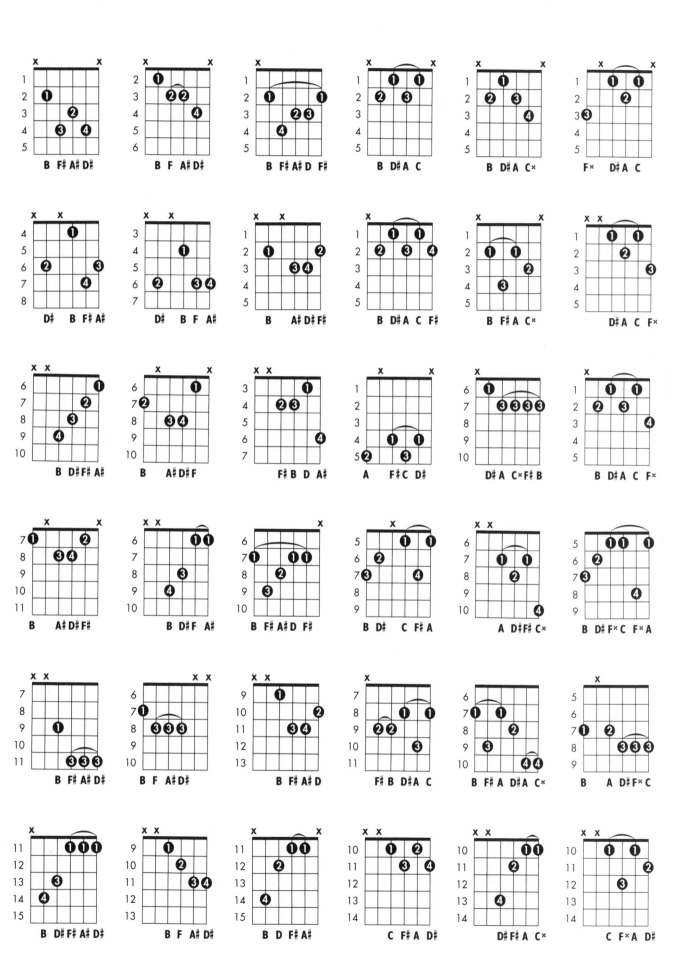

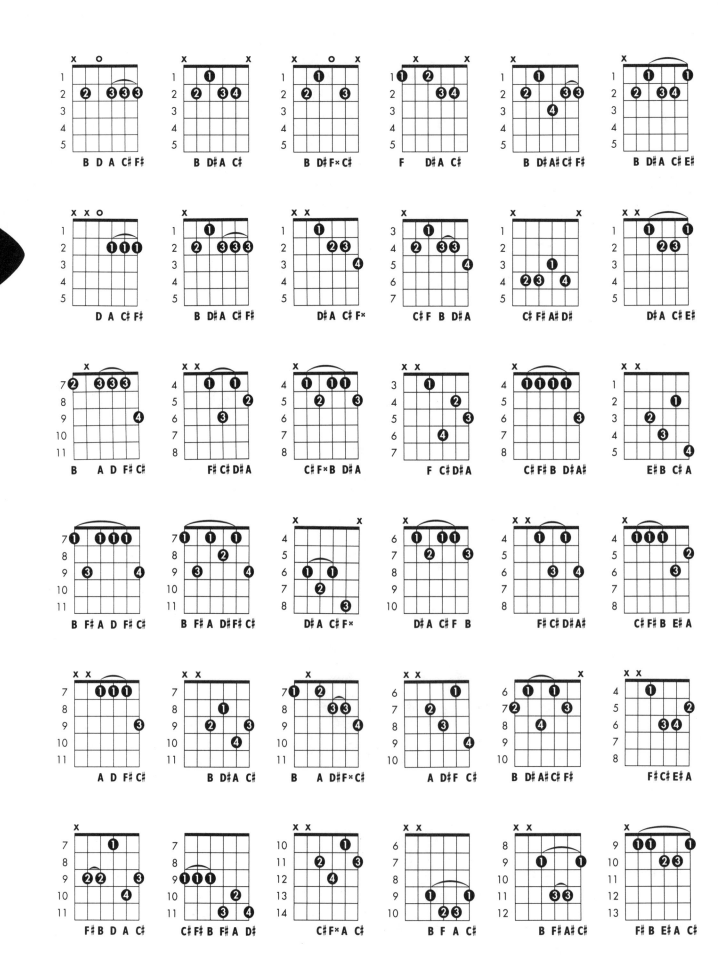

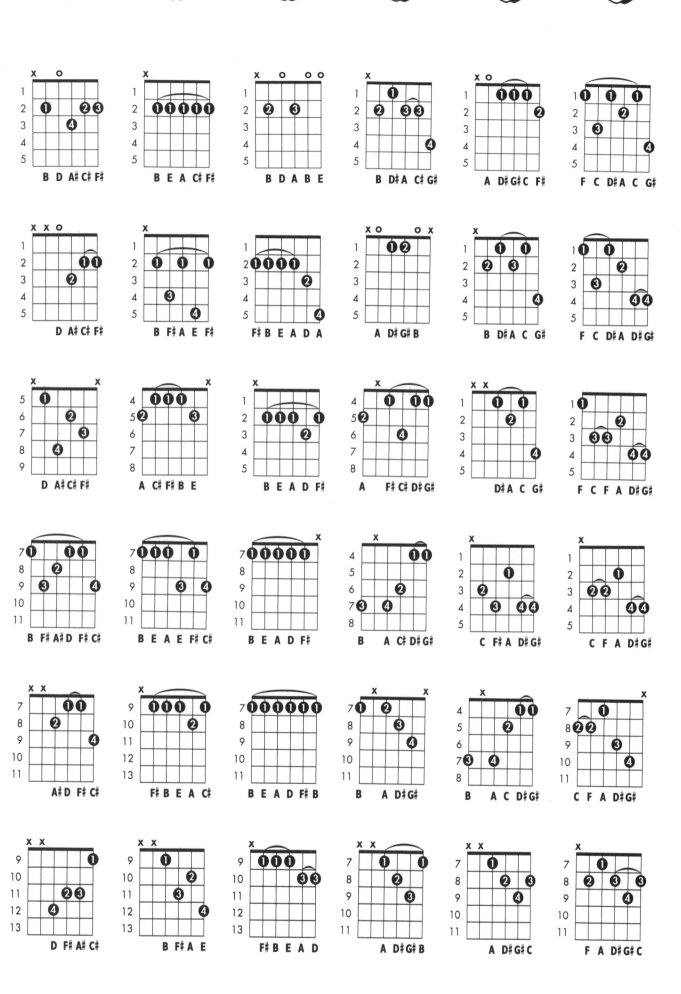

Bm9(maj7)    B11    Bm11    B13    B13(♭9)    B13(♭9/♭5)

B

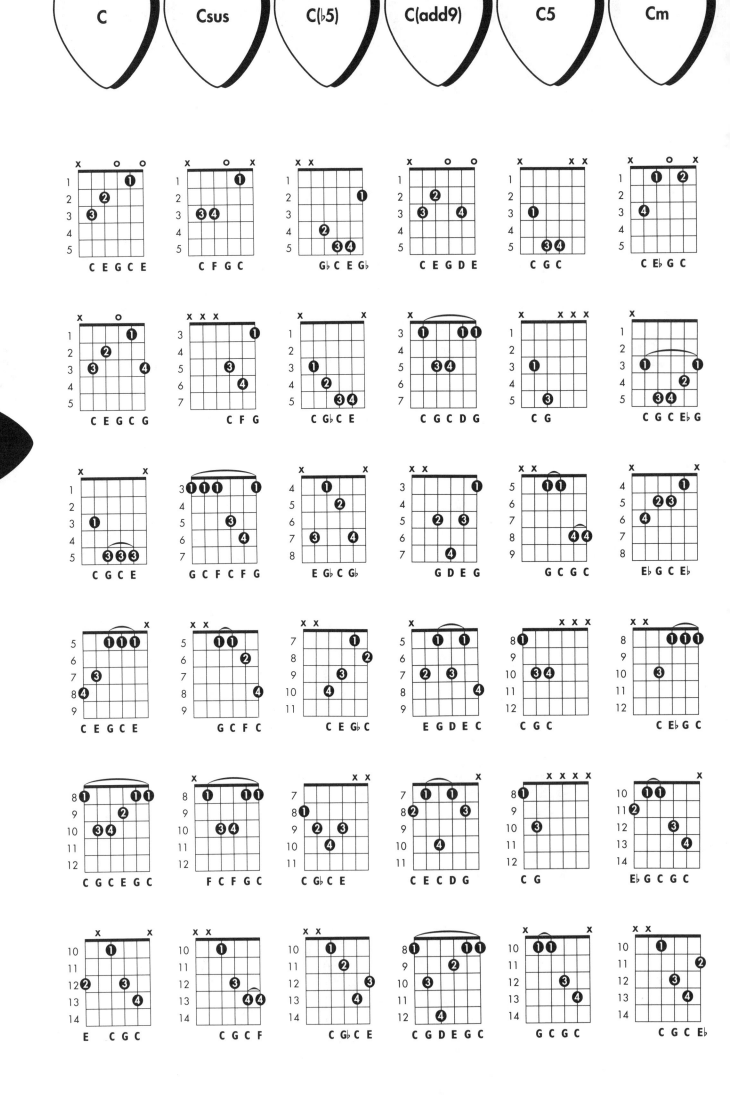

C    Csus    C(♭5)    C(add9)    C5    Cm

C

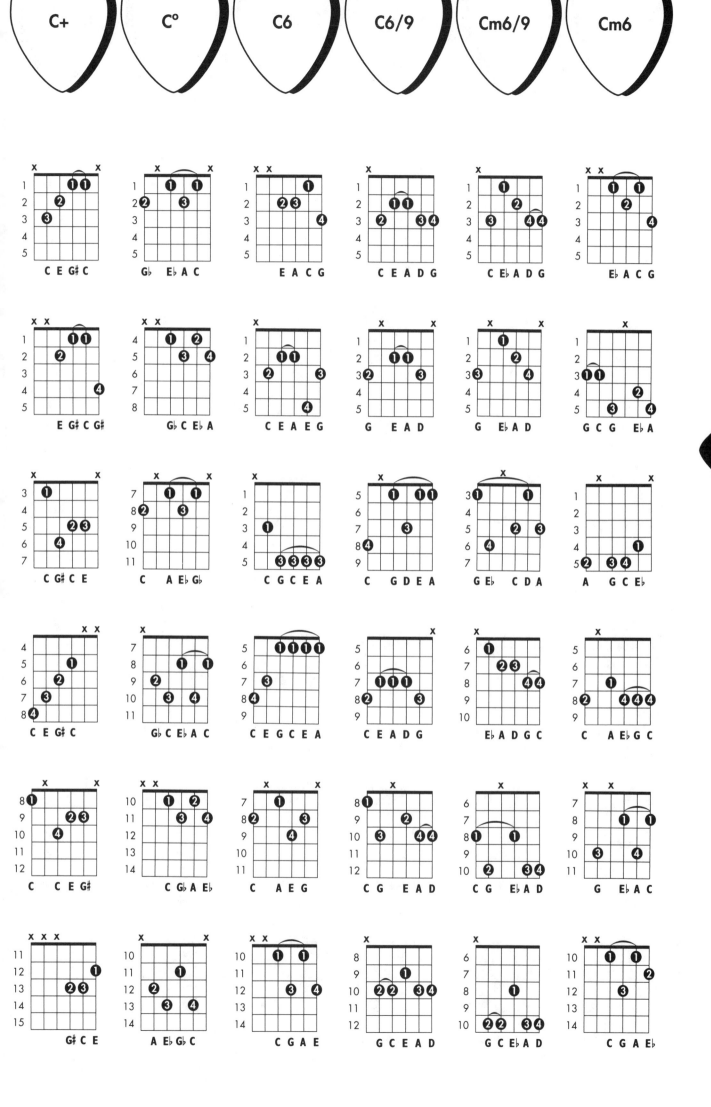

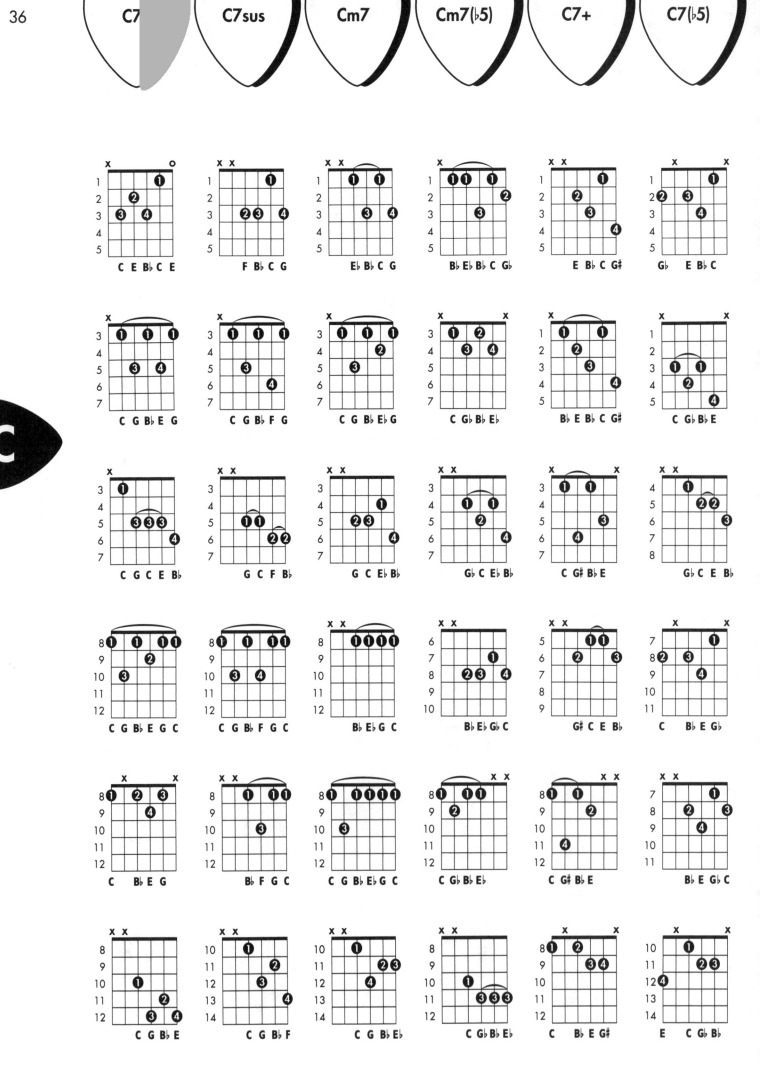

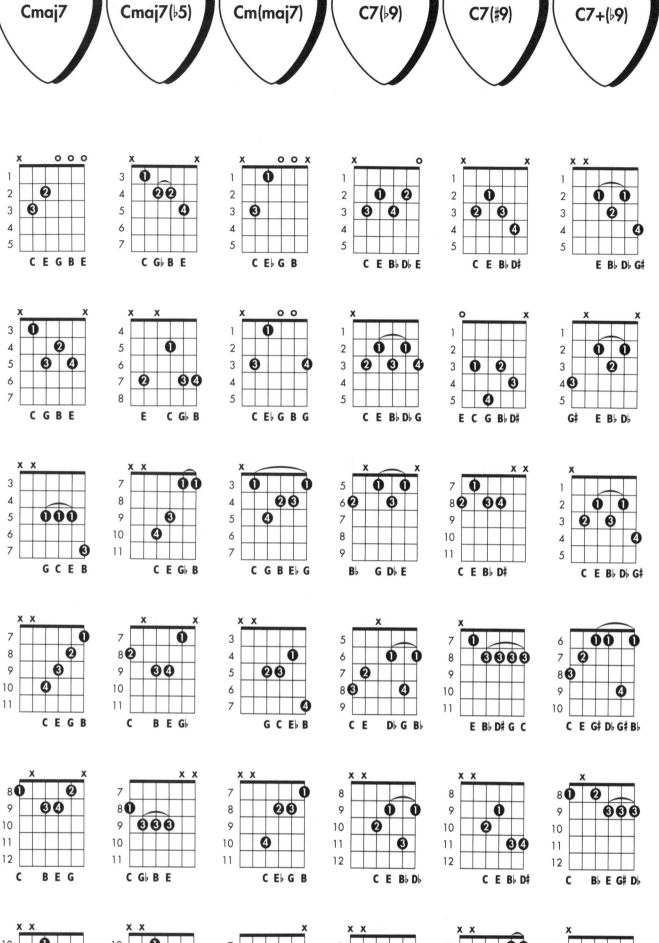

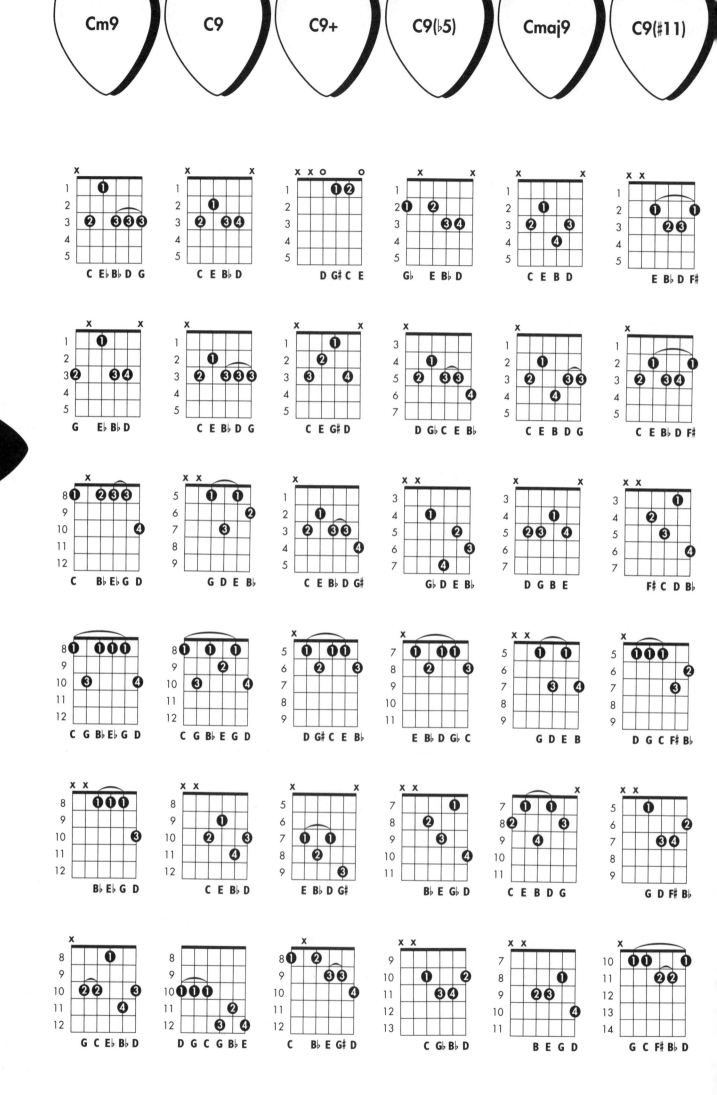

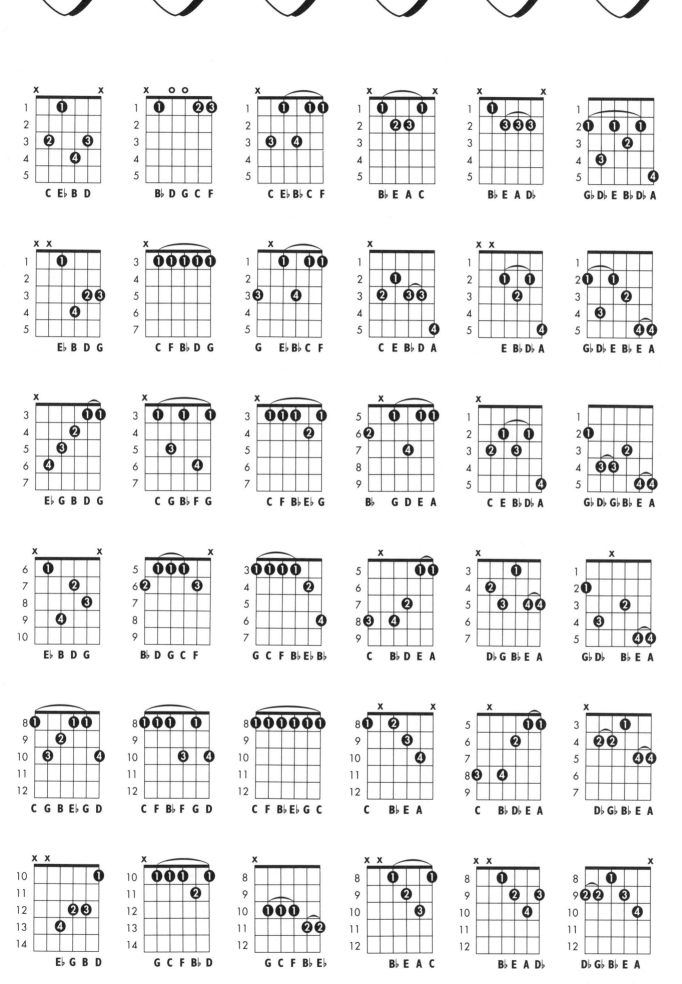

| Cm9(maj7) | C11 | Cm11 | C13 | C13(♭9) | C13(♭9♭5) |
|-----------|-----|------|-----|---------|-----------|

Row 1:
- C Eb B D
- Bb D G C F
- C Eb Bb C F
- Bb E A C
- Bb E A Db
- Gb Db E Bb Db A

Row 2:
- Eb B D G
- C F Bb D G
- G Eb Bb C F
- C E Bb D A
- E Bb Db A
- Gb Db E Bb E A

Row 3:
- Eb G B D G
- C G Bb F G
- C F Bb Eb G
- Bb G D E A
- C E Bb Db A
- Gb Db Gb Bb E A

Row 4:
- Eb B D G
- Bb D G C F
- G C F Bb Eb Bb
- C Bb D E A
- Db G Bb E A
- Gb Db Bb E A

Row 5:
- C G B Eb G D
- C F Bb F G D
- C F Bb Eb G C
- C Bb E A
- C Bb Db E A
- Db Gb Bb E A

Row 6:
- Eb G B D
- G C F Bb D
- G C F Bb Eb
- Bb E A C
- Bb E A Db
- Db Gb Bb E A

C

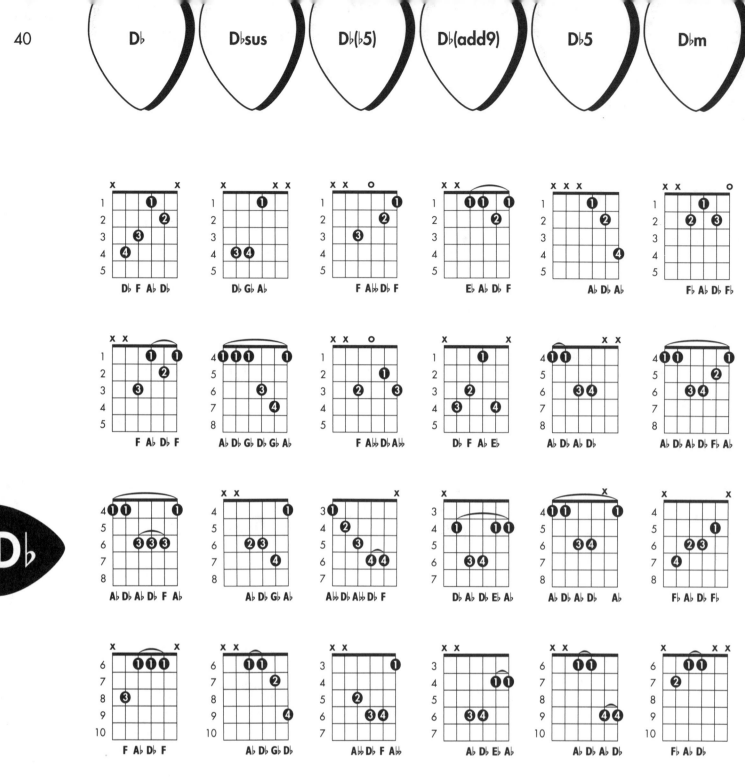

**D♭**    **D♭sus**    **D♭(♭5)**    **D♭(add9)**    **D♭5**    **D♭m**

D♭

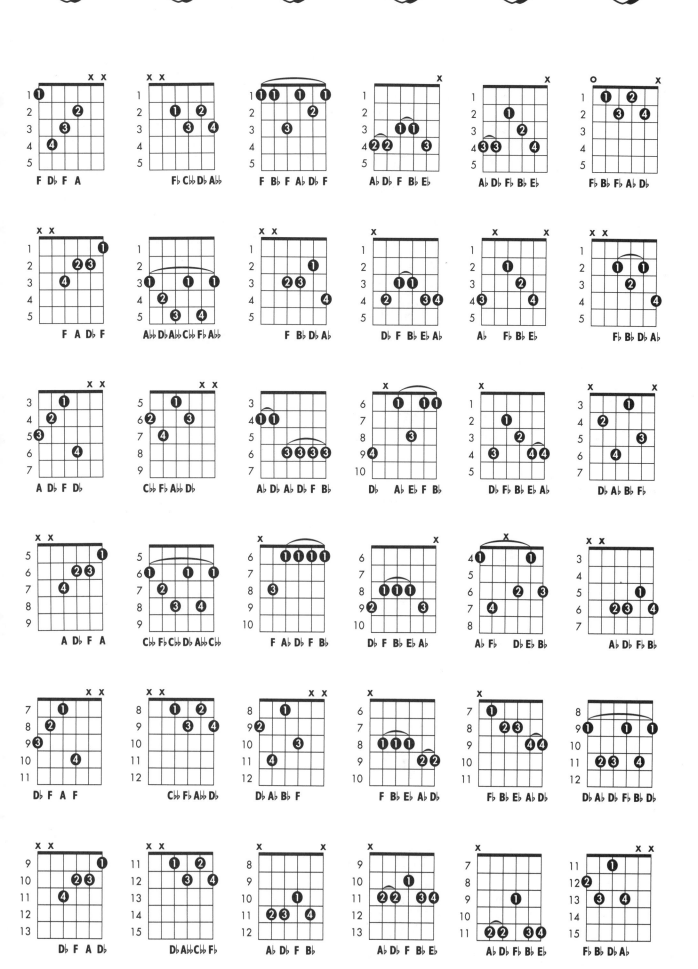

Db+    Db°    Db6    Db6/9    Dbm6/9    Dbm6

Db

# Db7 · Db7sus · Dbm7 · Dbm7(b5) · Db7+ · Db7(b5)

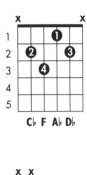

**Db**

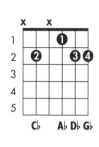 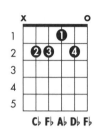 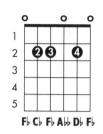 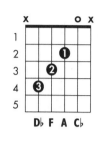 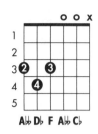

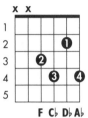 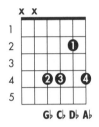 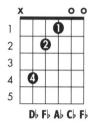 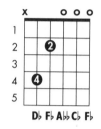 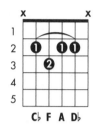 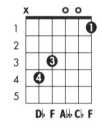

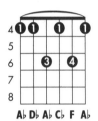 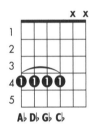 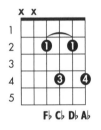 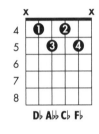 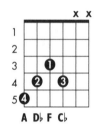 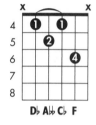

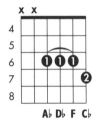 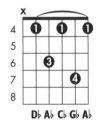  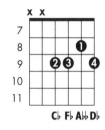 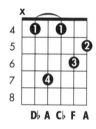 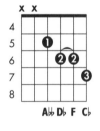

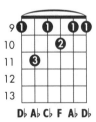 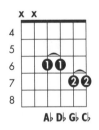 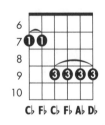 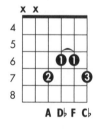 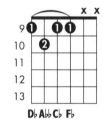 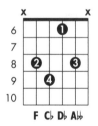

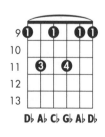 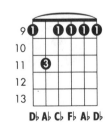 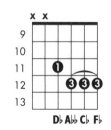 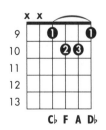 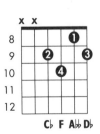

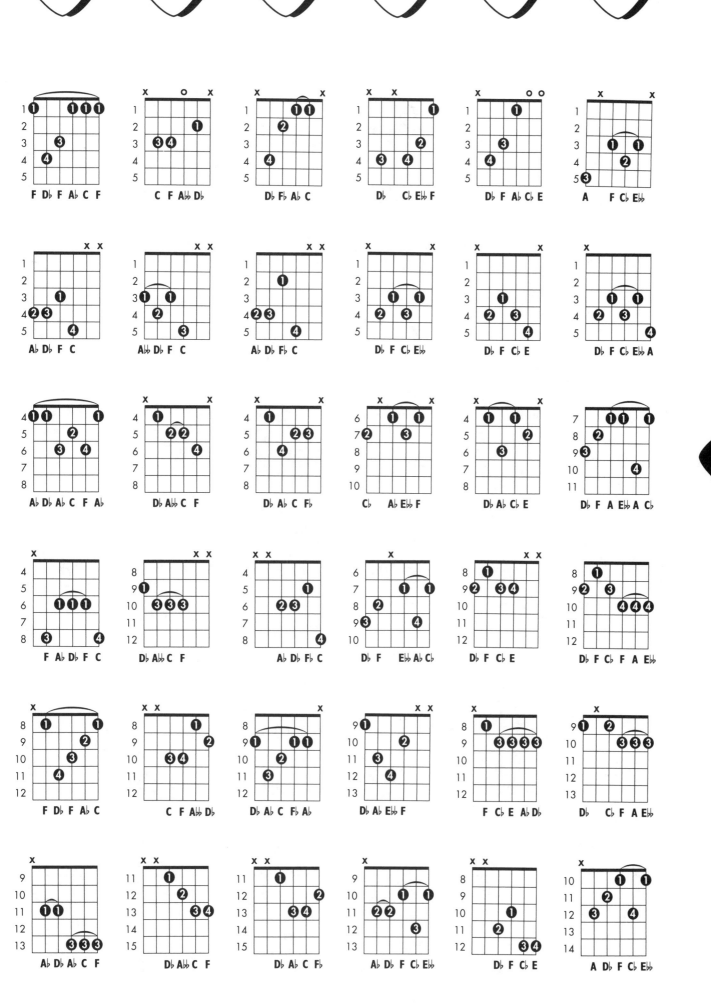

D♭maj7    D♭maj7(♭5)    D♭m(maj7)    D♭7(♭9)    D♭7(♯9)    D♭7+(♭9)

D♭

**D♭m9**  **D♭9**  **D♭9+**  **D♭9(♭5)**  **D♭maj9**  **D♭9(#11)**

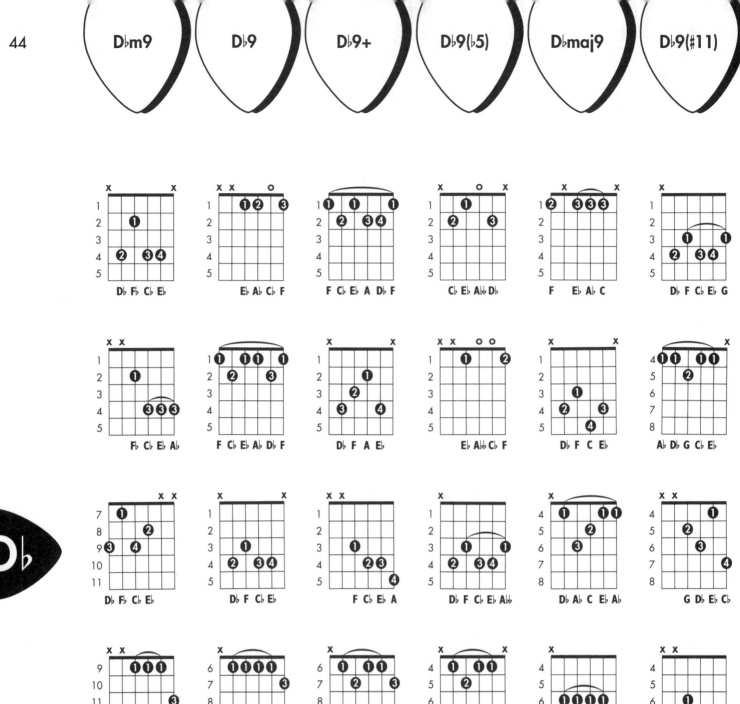
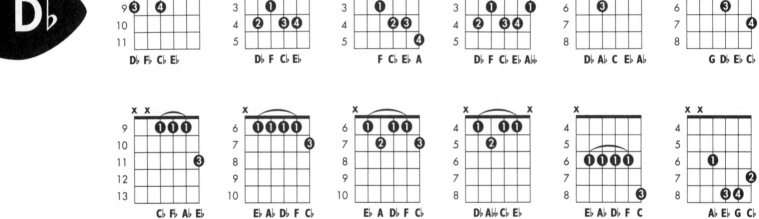
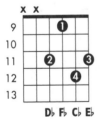
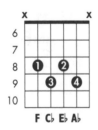
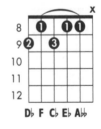
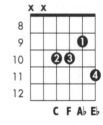
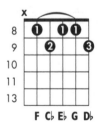
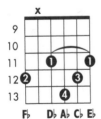
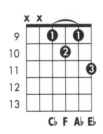
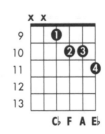
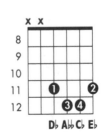
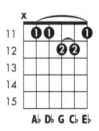

D♭

| D♭m9(maj7) | D♭11 | D♭m11 | D♭13 | D♭13(♭9) | D♭13(♭9/♭5) |
|---|---|---|---|---|---|

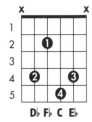 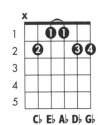 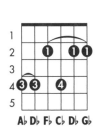 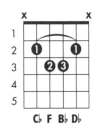 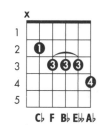 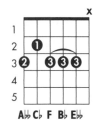

D♭ F♭ C E♭ — C♭ E♭ A♭ D♭ G♭ — A♭ D♭ F♭ C♭ D♭ G♭ — C♭ F B♭ D♭ — C♭ F B♭ E♭ A♭ — A♭♭ C♭ F B♭ E♭♭

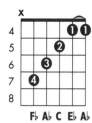  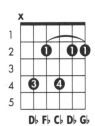 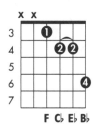 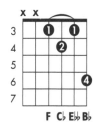 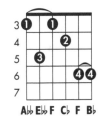

F♭ A♭ C E♭ A♭ — A♭ D♭ G♭ C♭ E♭ A♭ — D♭ F♭ C♭ D♭ G♭ — F C♭ E♭ B♭ — F C♭ E♭♭ B♭ — A♭♭ E♭♭ F C♭ F B♭

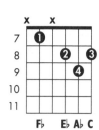 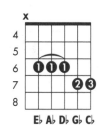 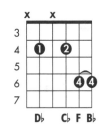 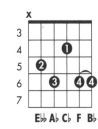 

F♭ E♭ A♭ C — E♭ A♭ D♭ G♭ C♭ — D♭ G♭ C♭ F♭ A♭ — D♭ C♭ F B♭ — E♭♭ A♭ C♭ F B♭ — A♭♭ E♭♭ F C♭ E♭♭ B♭

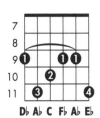 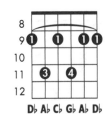  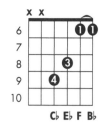 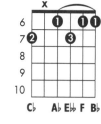 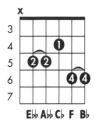

D♭ F♭ C E♭ — D♭ G♭ C♭ E♭ — A♭ D♭ G♭ C♭ F♭ C♭ — C♭ E♭ F B♭ — C♭ A♭ E♭♭ F B♭ — A♭ E♭♭ A♭♭ C♭ F B♭

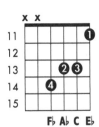 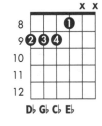 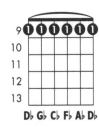 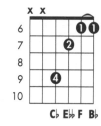 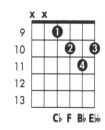 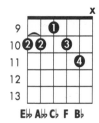

D♭ A♭ C F♭ A♭ E♭ — D♭ A♭ C♭ G♭ A♭ D♭ — D♭ G♭ C♭ F♭ A♭ D♭ — C♭ F B♭ D♭ — C♭ E♭♭ F B♭ — E♭♭ A♭♭ C♭ F B♭

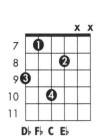 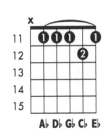 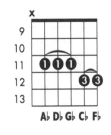 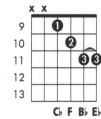 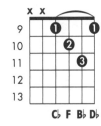 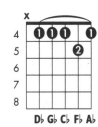 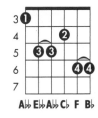

F♭ A♭ C E♭ — A♭ D♭ G♭ C♭ E♭ — A♭ D♭ G♭ C♭ F♭ — C♭ F B♭ E♭ — C♭ F B♭ E♭♭ — E♭♭ A♭♭ C♭ F B♭

D♭

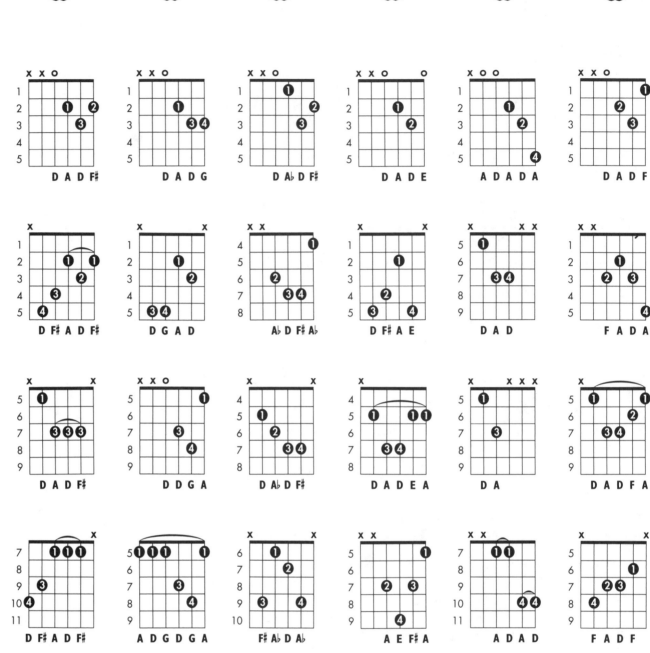

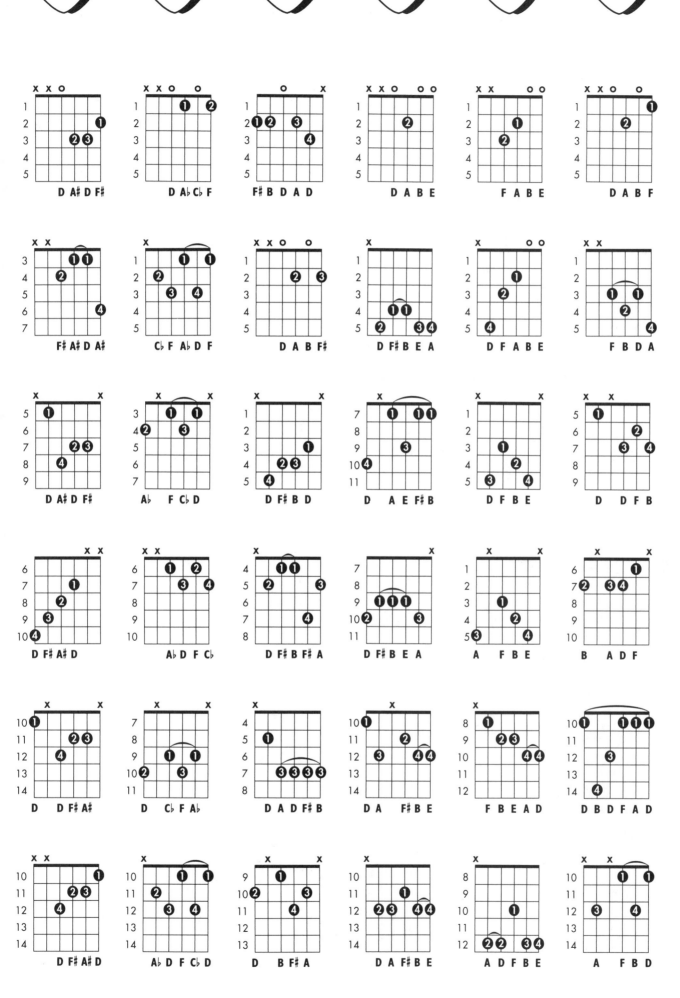

D+ | D° | D6 | D6/9 | Dm6/9 | Dm6

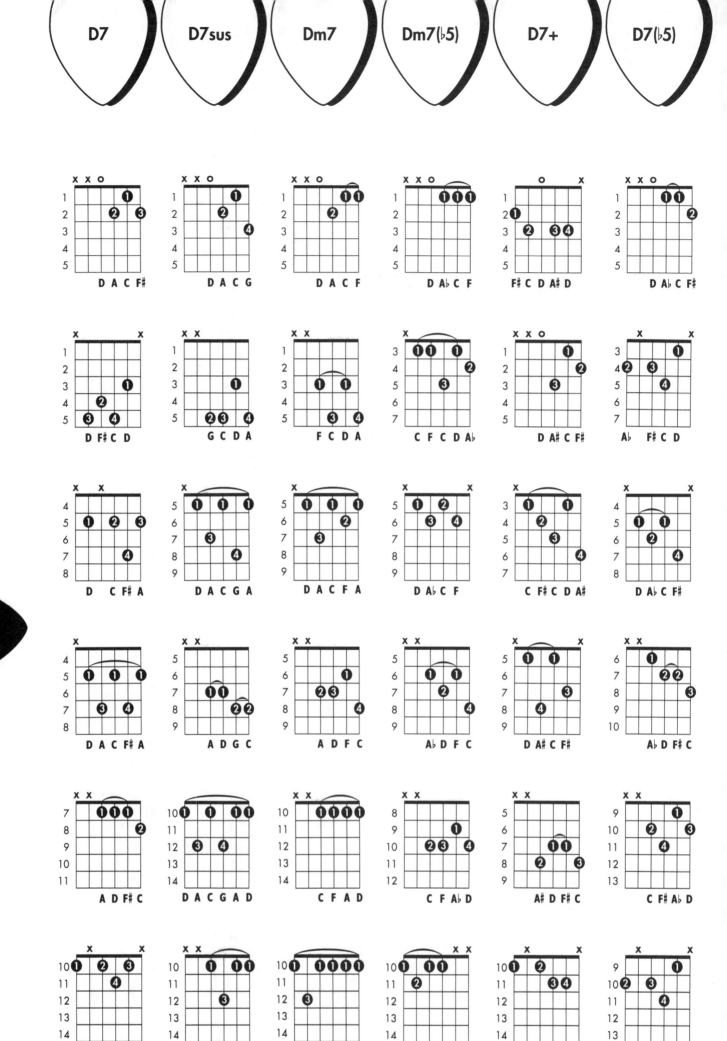

D7   D7sus   Dm7   Dm7(♭5)   D7+   D7(♭5)

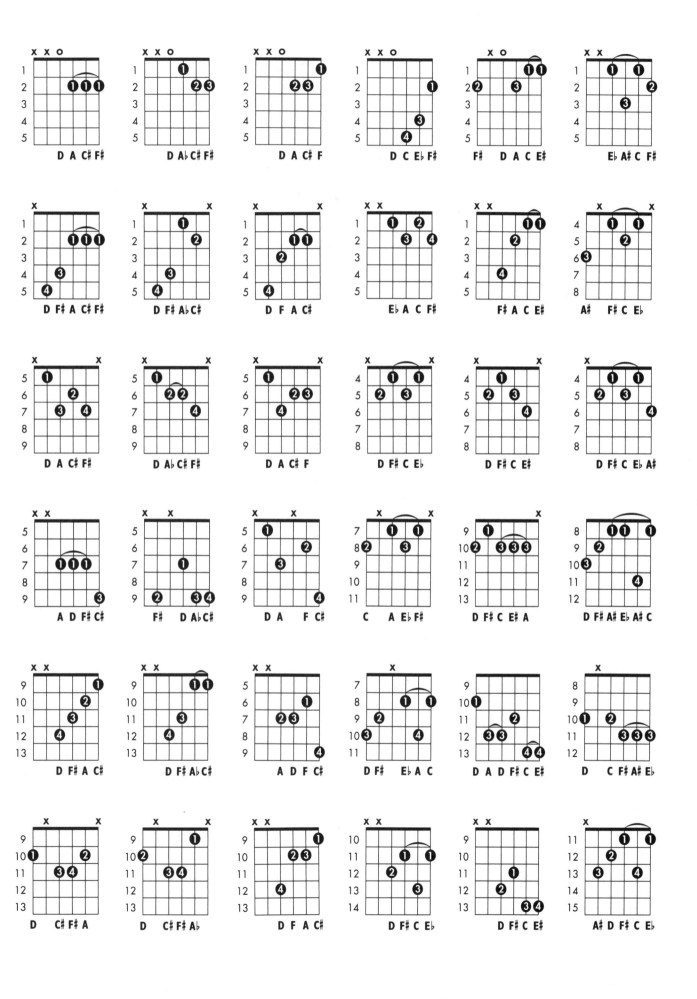

Dmaj7 | Dmaj7(♭5) | Dm(maj7) | D7(♭9) | D7(#9) | D7+(♭9)

**D**

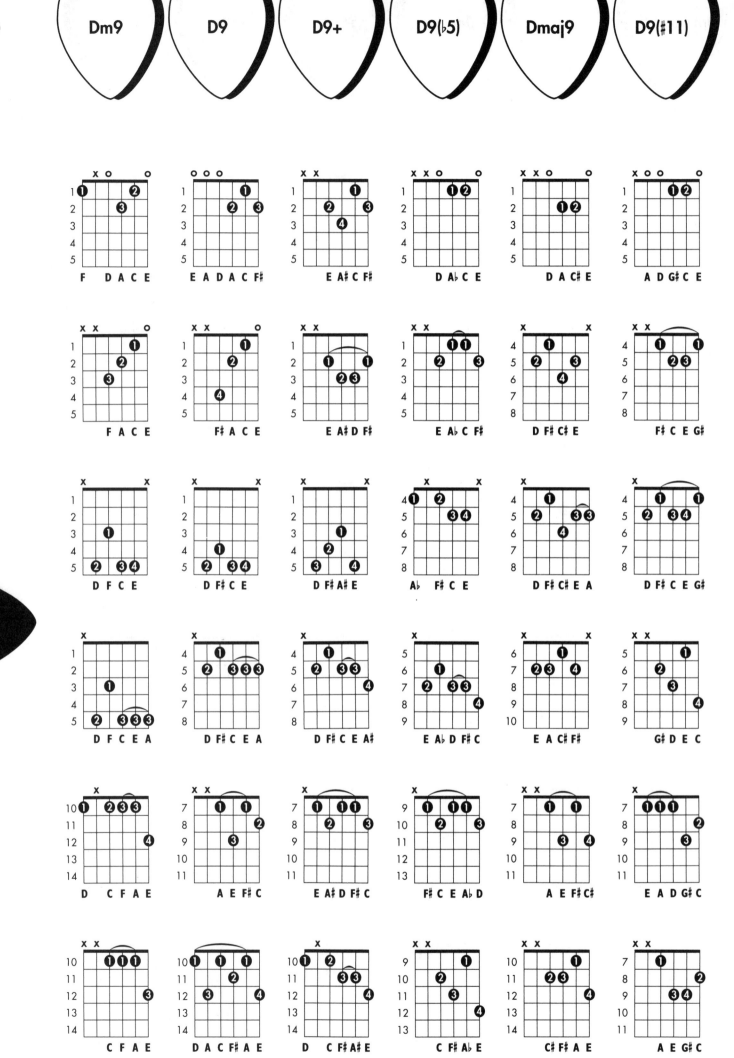

## Dm9(maj7) | D11 | Dm11 | D13 | D13(♭9) | D13(♭9 ♭5)

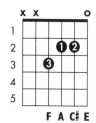 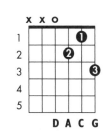 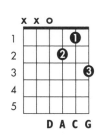 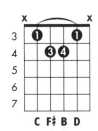 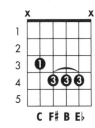 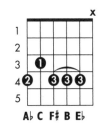

F A C♯ E | D A C G | D A C G | C F♯ B D | C F♯ B E♭ | A♭ C F♯ B E♭

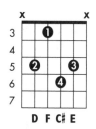 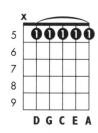 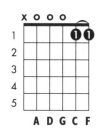 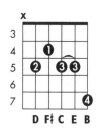 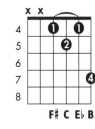 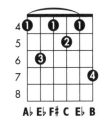

D F C♯ E | D G C E A | A D G C F | D F♯ C E B | F♯ C E♭ B | A♭ E♭ F♯ C E♭ B

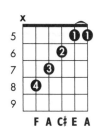 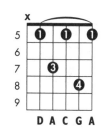 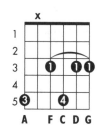 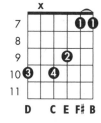 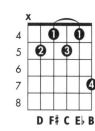 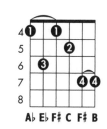

F A C♯ E A | D A C G A | A F C D G | D C E F♯ B | D F♯ C E♭ B | A♭ E♭ F♯ C F♯ B

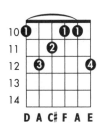 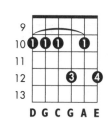  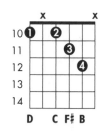 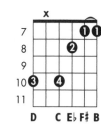 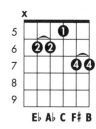

F C♯ E A | C E A D G | D G C F A | C A E F♯ B | E♭ A C F♯ B | A♭ E♭ A♭ C F♯ B

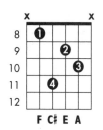 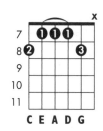 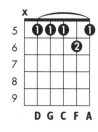 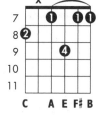  

D A C♯ F A E | D G C G A E | A D G C F C | D C F♯ B | D C E♭ F♯ B | E♭ A♭ C F♯ B

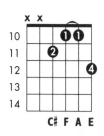 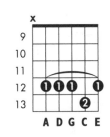 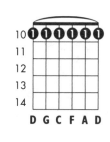 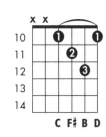 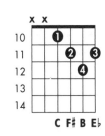 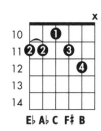

C♯ F A E | A D G C E | D G C F A D | C F♯ B D | C F♯ B E♭ | E♭ A♭ C F♯ B

**D**

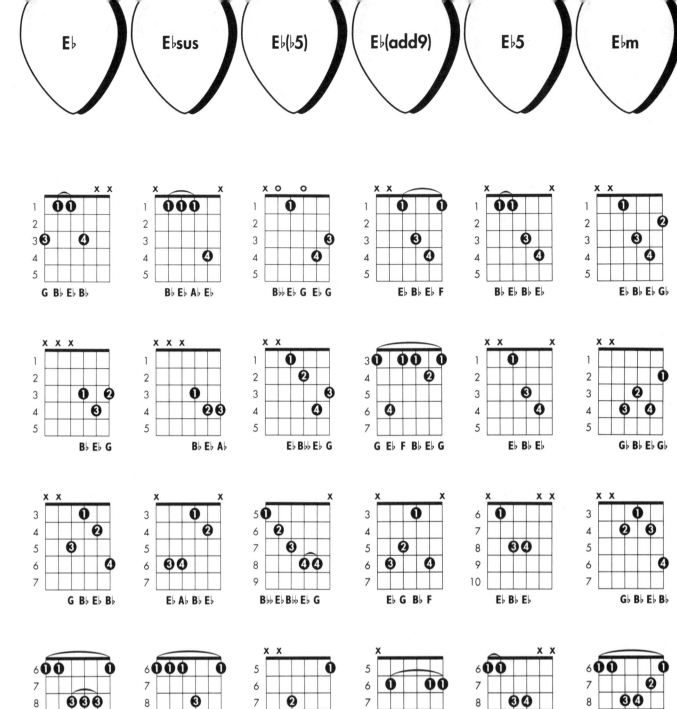

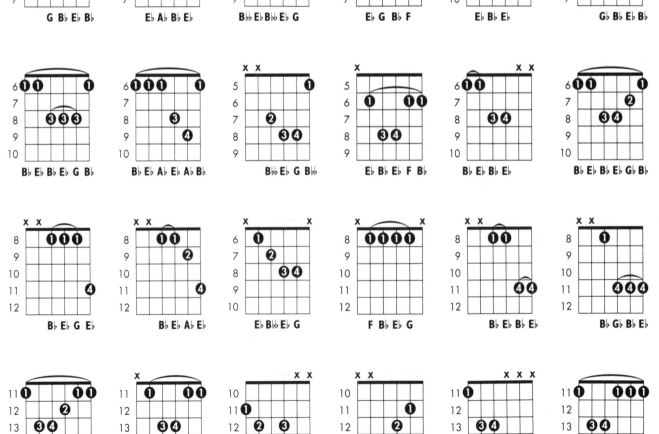

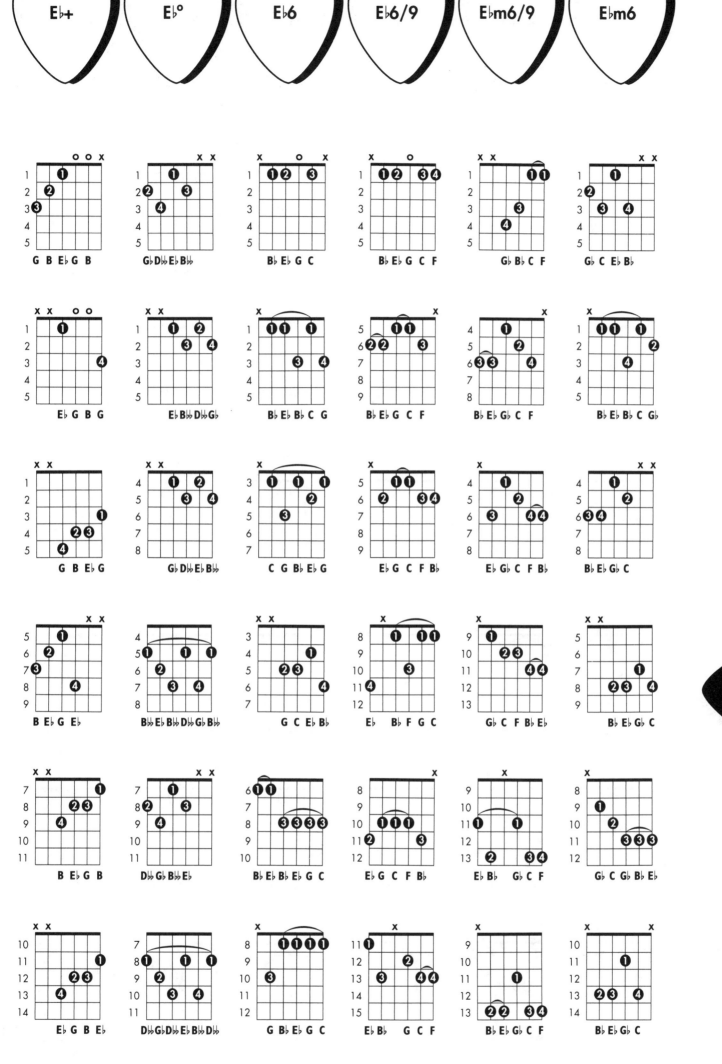

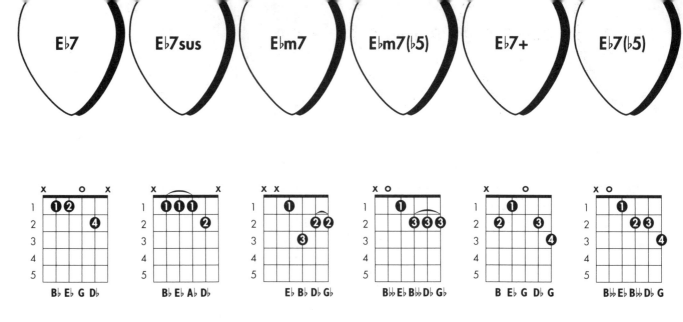

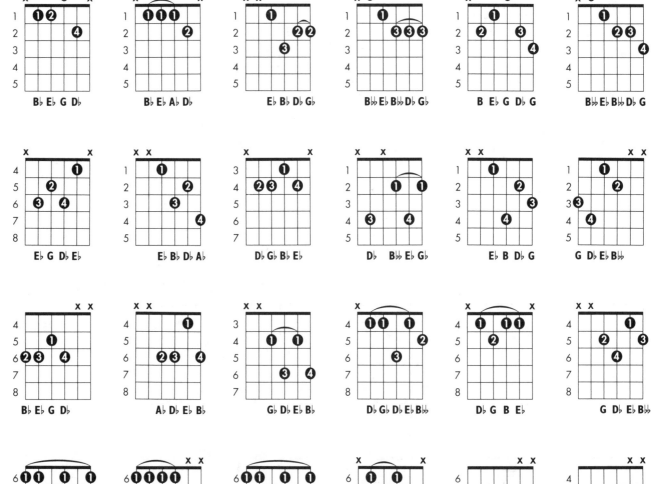

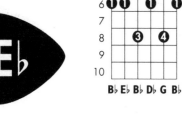

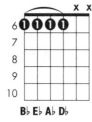
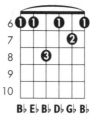
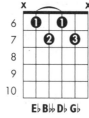
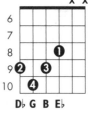
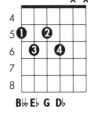

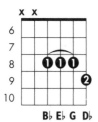
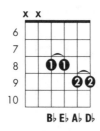
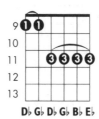
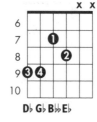
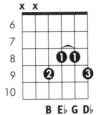
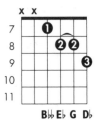

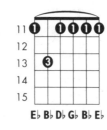
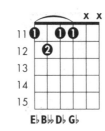
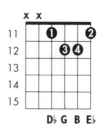
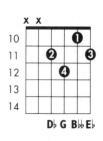

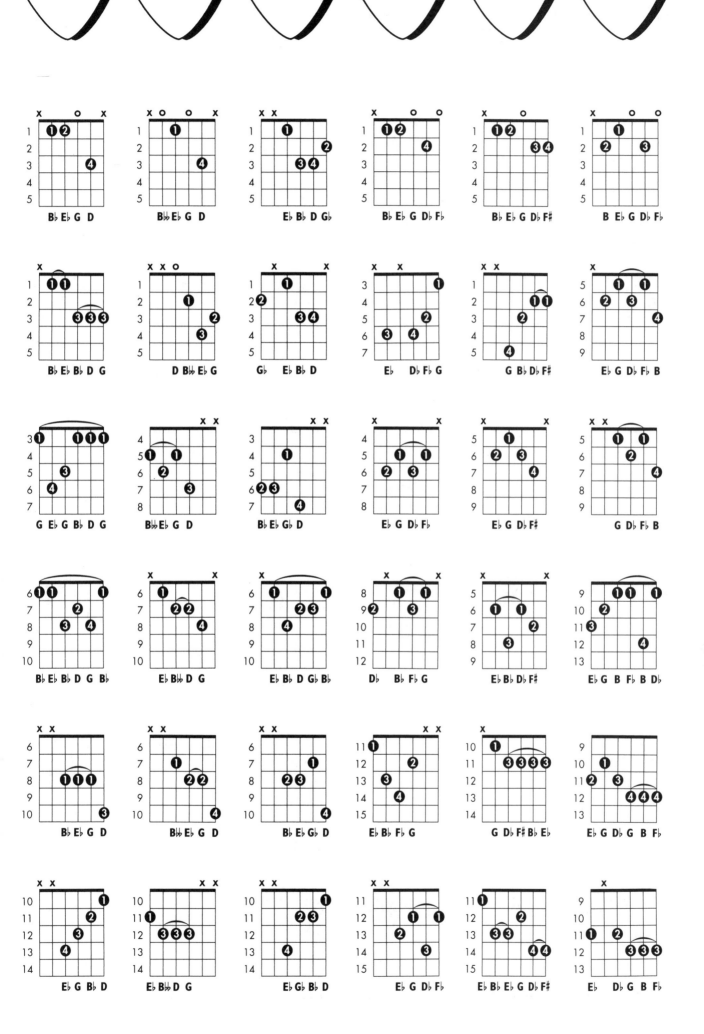

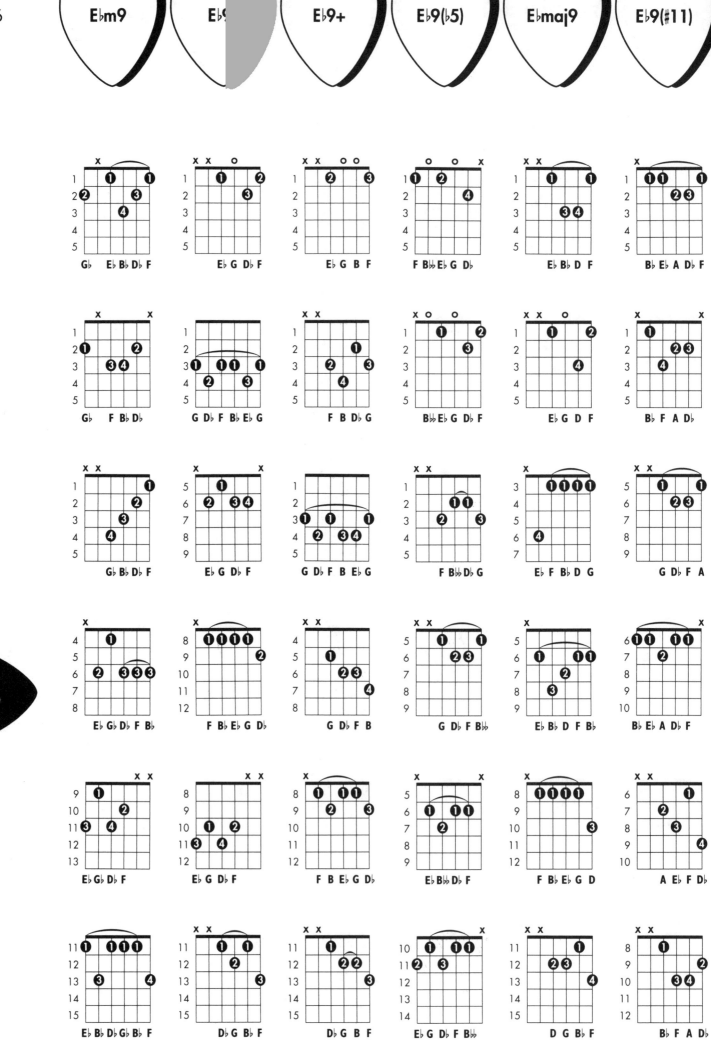

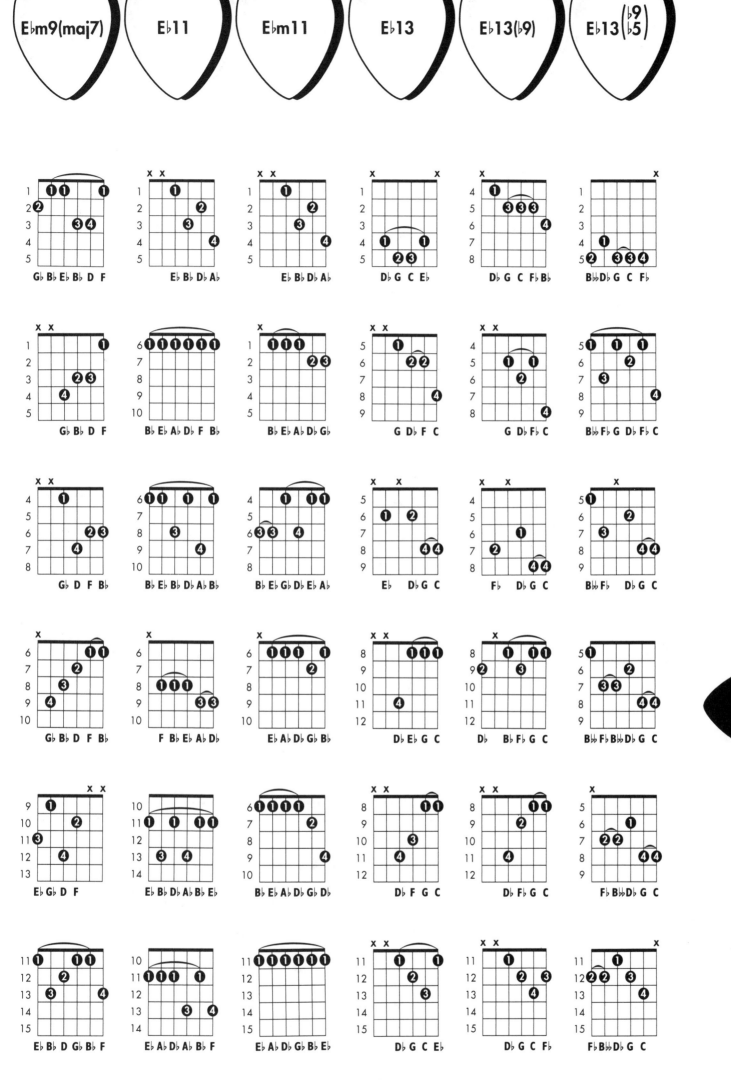

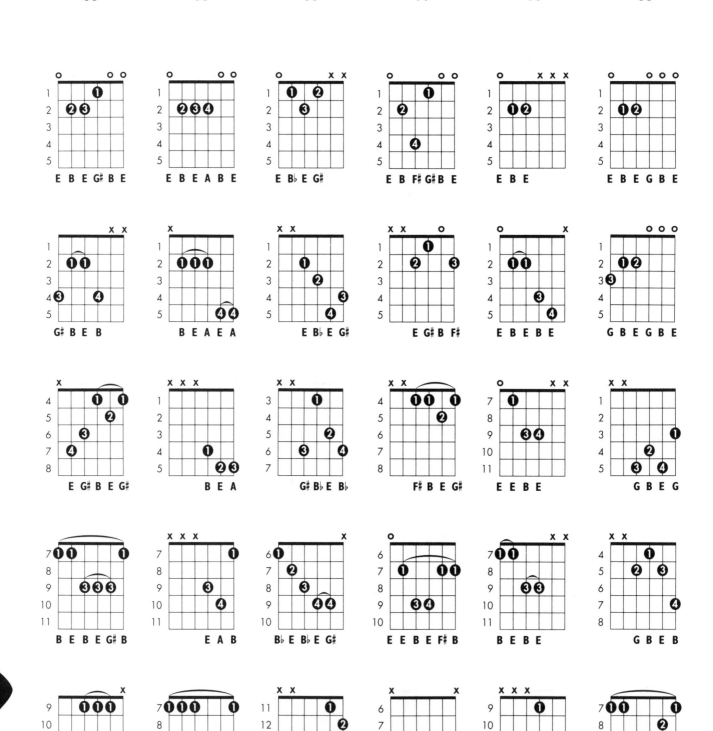

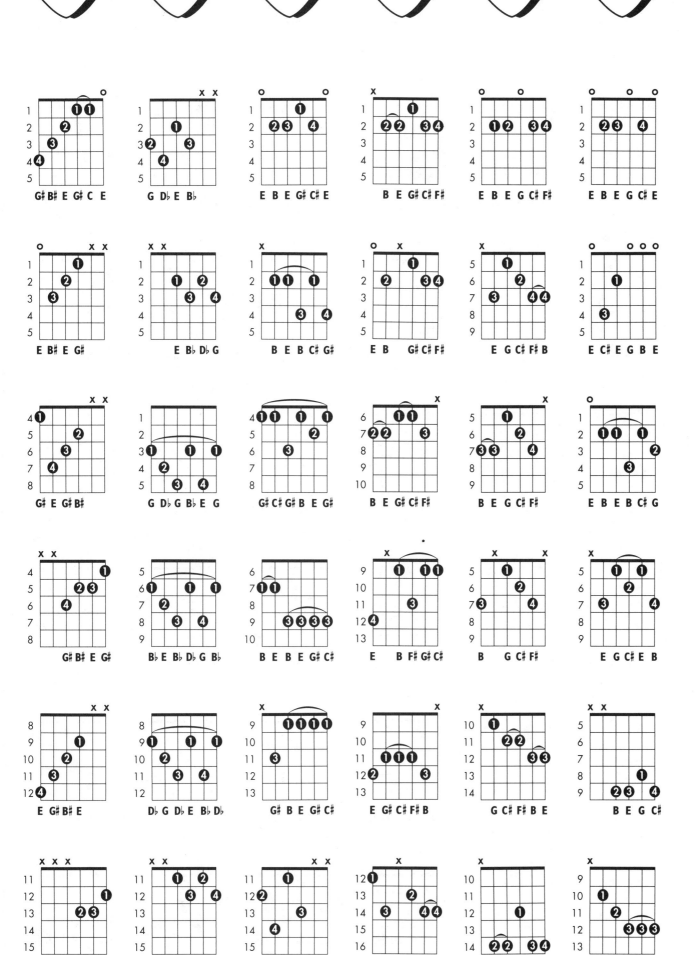

E+   E°   E6   E6/9   Em6/9   Em6

E

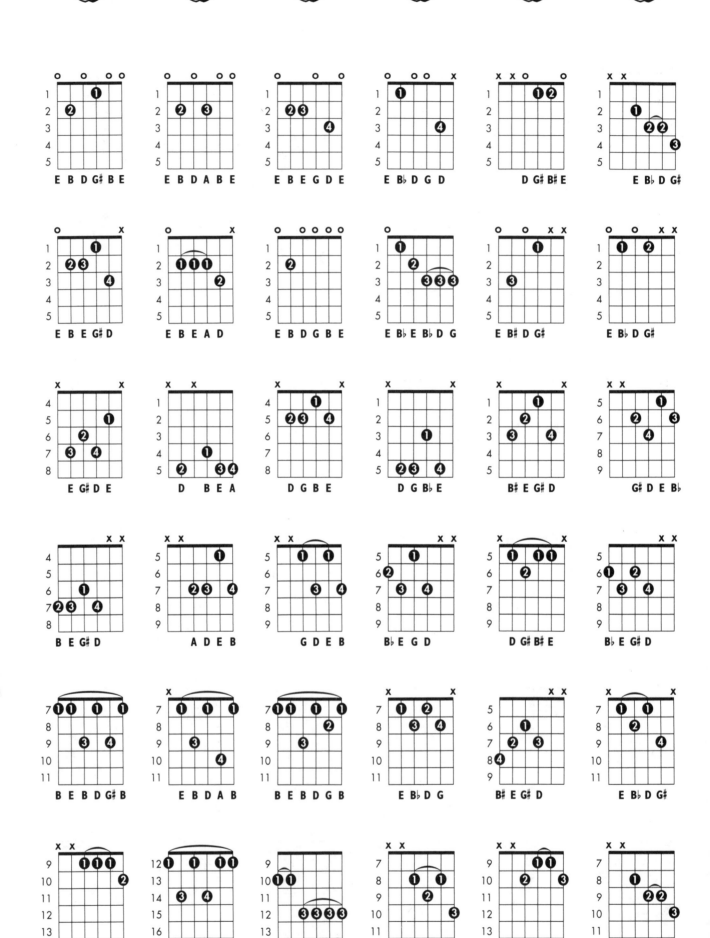

# Emaj7   Emaj7(♭5)   Em(maj7)   E7(♭9)   E7(#9)   E7+(♭9)

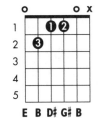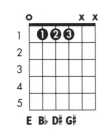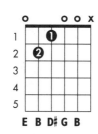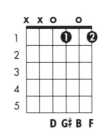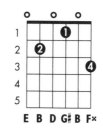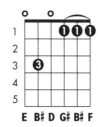

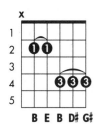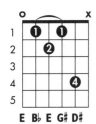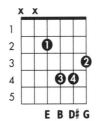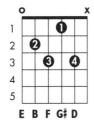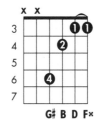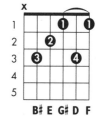

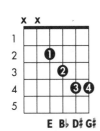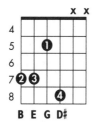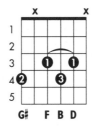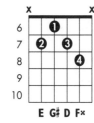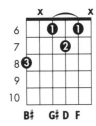

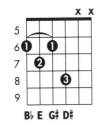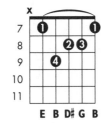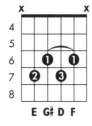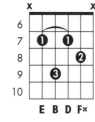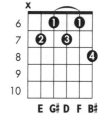

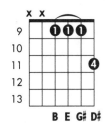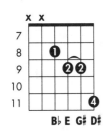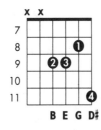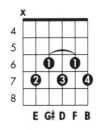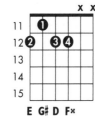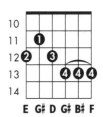

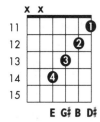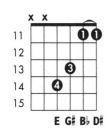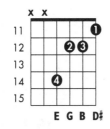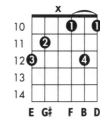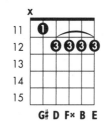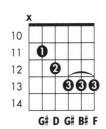

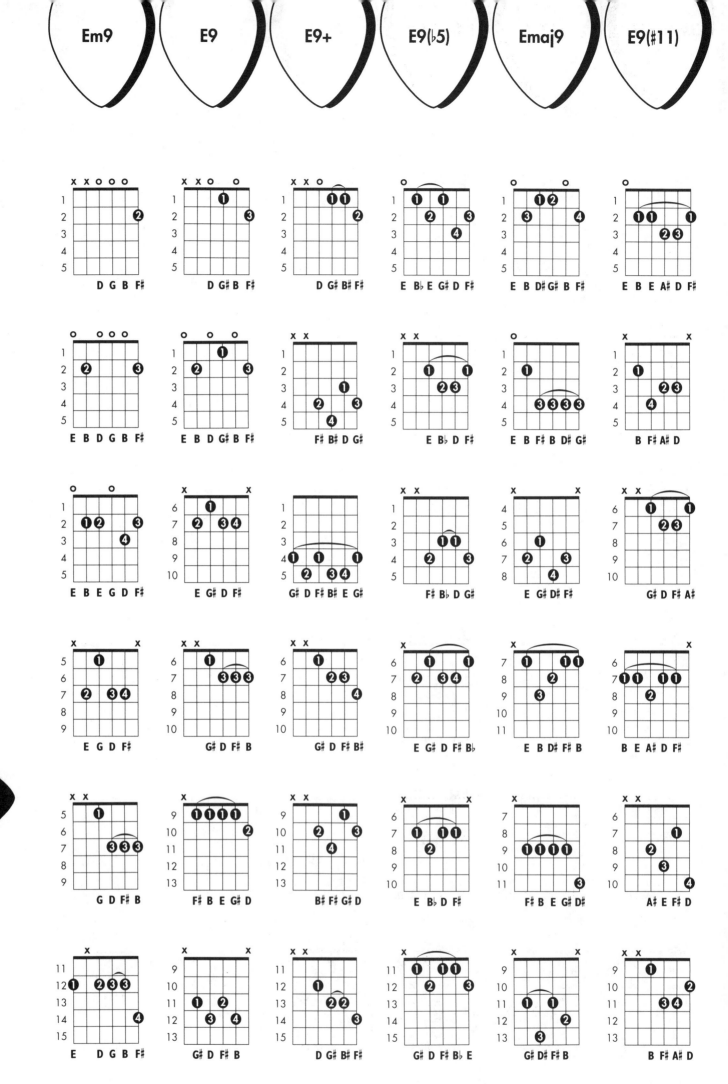

E

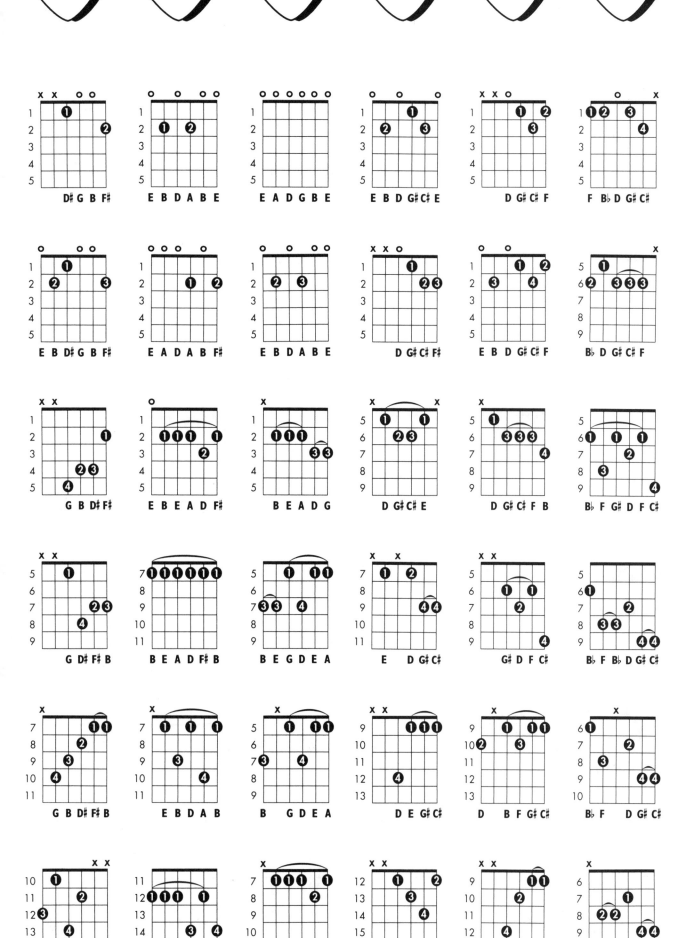

Em9(maj7)  E11  Em11  E13  E13(♭9)  E13$\binom{♭9}{♭5}$

63

E

F  Fsus  F(♭5)  F(add9)  F5  Fm

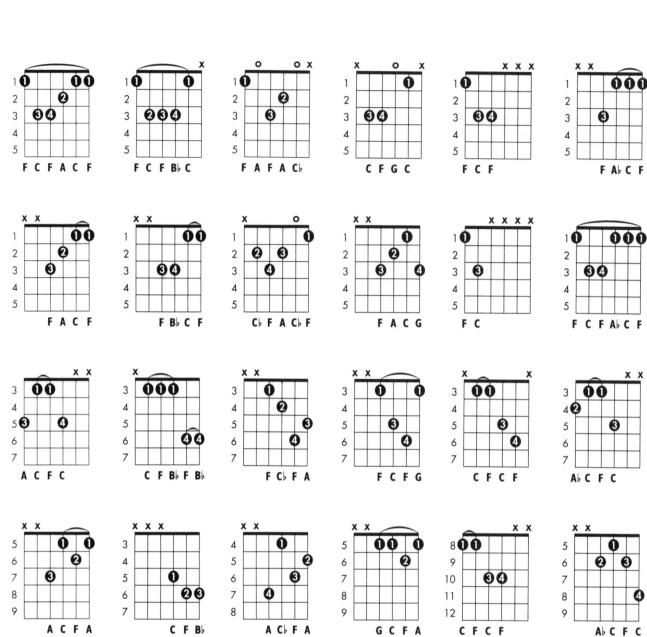
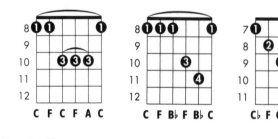
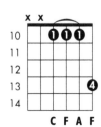
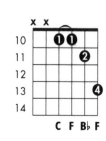
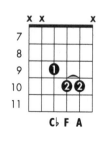
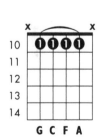
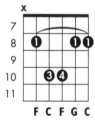
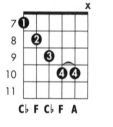
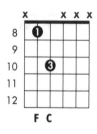
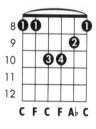
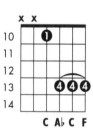
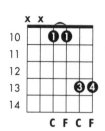

F

| F+ | F° | F6 | F6/9 | Fm6/9 | Fm6 |

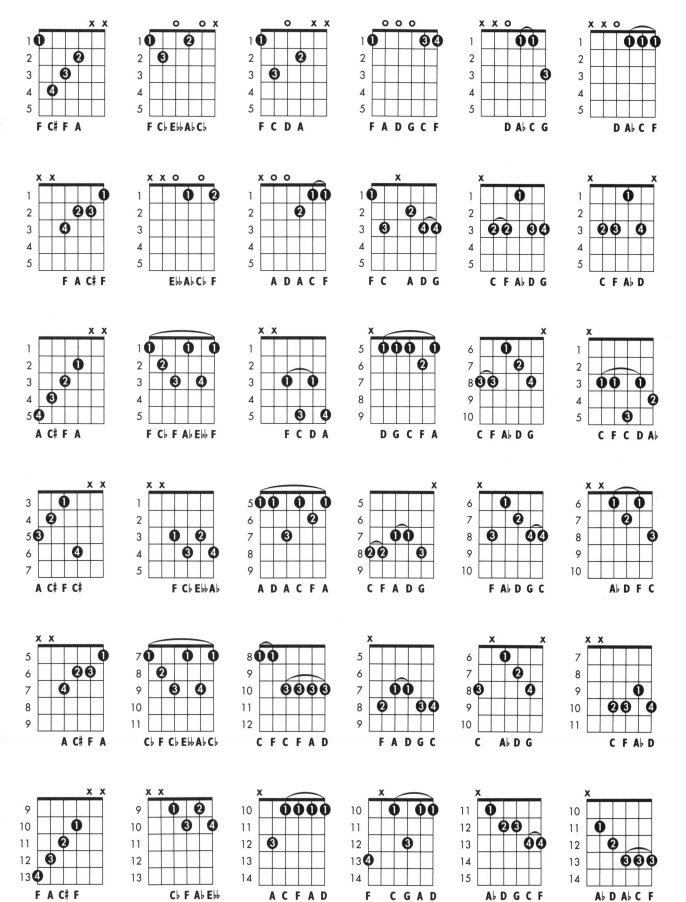

F

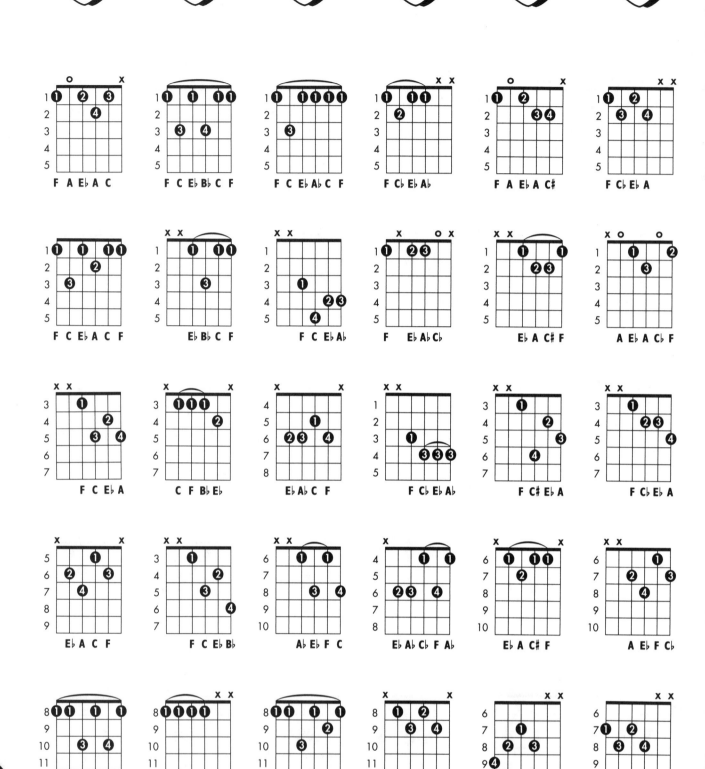

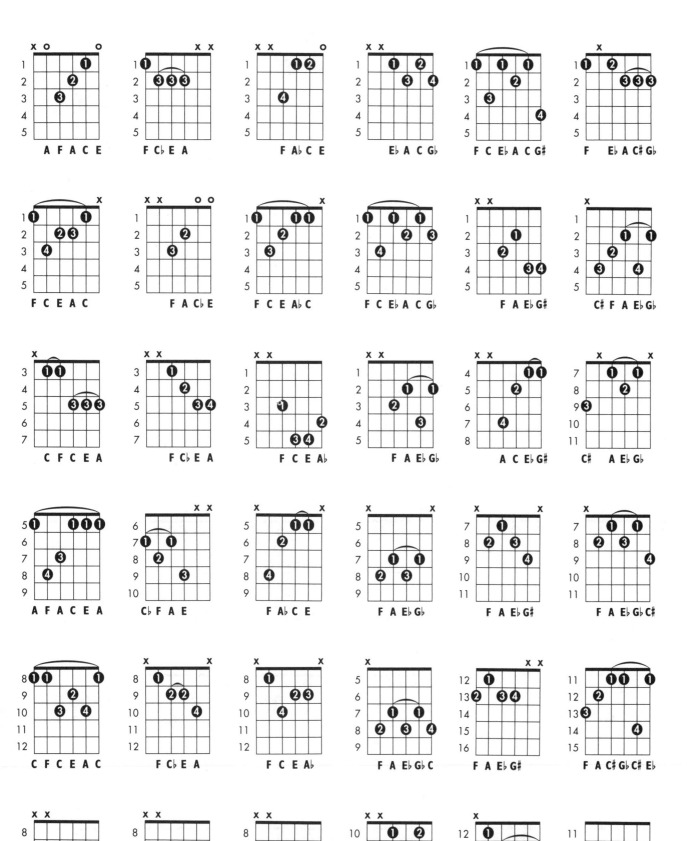

**Fm9**   **F9**   **F9+**   **F9(♭5)**   **Fmaj9**   **F9(#11)**

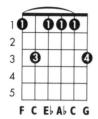 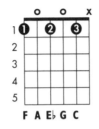 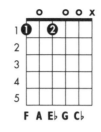 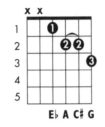 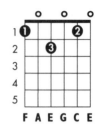 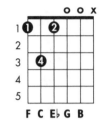

| Fm9 | F9 | F9+ | F9(♭5) | Fmaj9 | F9(#11) |
|---|---|---|---|---|---|
| F C E♭ A♭ C G | F A E♭ G C | A E♭ G C# F | F A E♭ G C♭ | F A E G C E | F C E♭ G B |

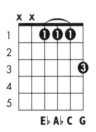 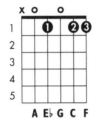 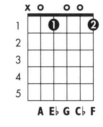 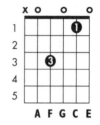 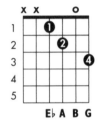 

| E♭ A♭ C G | A E♭ G C F | E♭ A C# G | A E♭ G C♭ F | A F G C E | E♭ A B G |

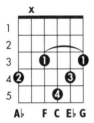 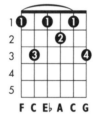 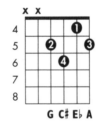 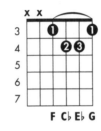 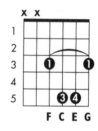 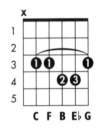

| A♭ F C E♭ G | F C E♭ A C G | G C# E♭ A | F C♭ E♭ G | F C E G | C F B E♭ G |

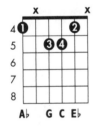 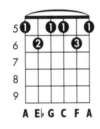 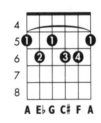 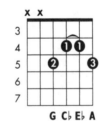 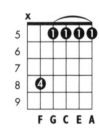 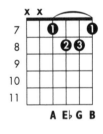

| A♭ G C E♭ | A E♭ G C F A | A E♭ G C# F A | G C♭ E♭ A | F G C E A | A E♭ G B |

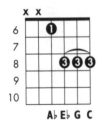 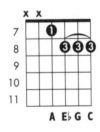 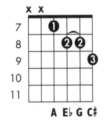 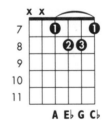 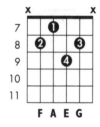 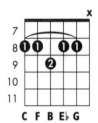

| A♭ E♭ G C | A E♭ G C | A E♭ G C# | A E♭ G C♭ | F A E G | C F B E♭ G |

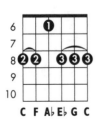 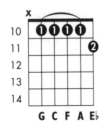 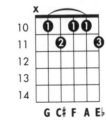 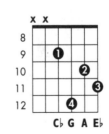 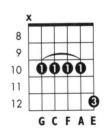 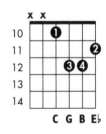

| C F A♭ E♭ G C | G C F A E♭ | G C# F A E♭ | C♭ G A E♭ | G C F A E | C G B E♭ |

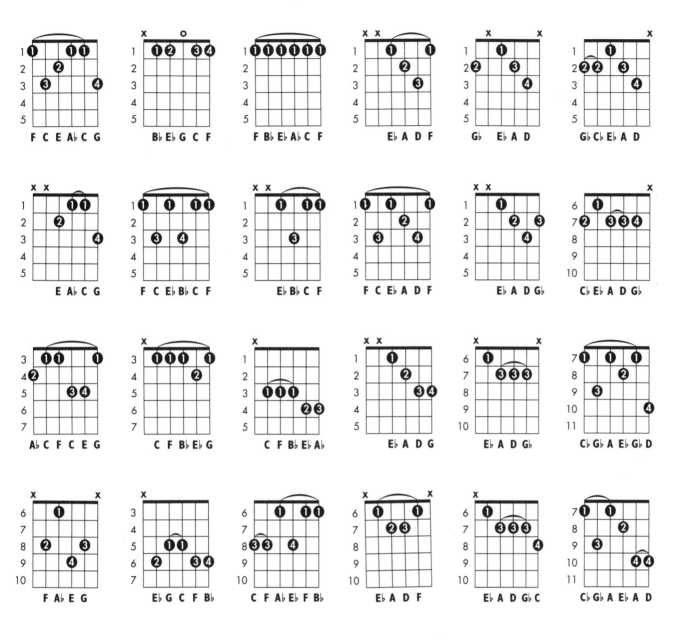

F

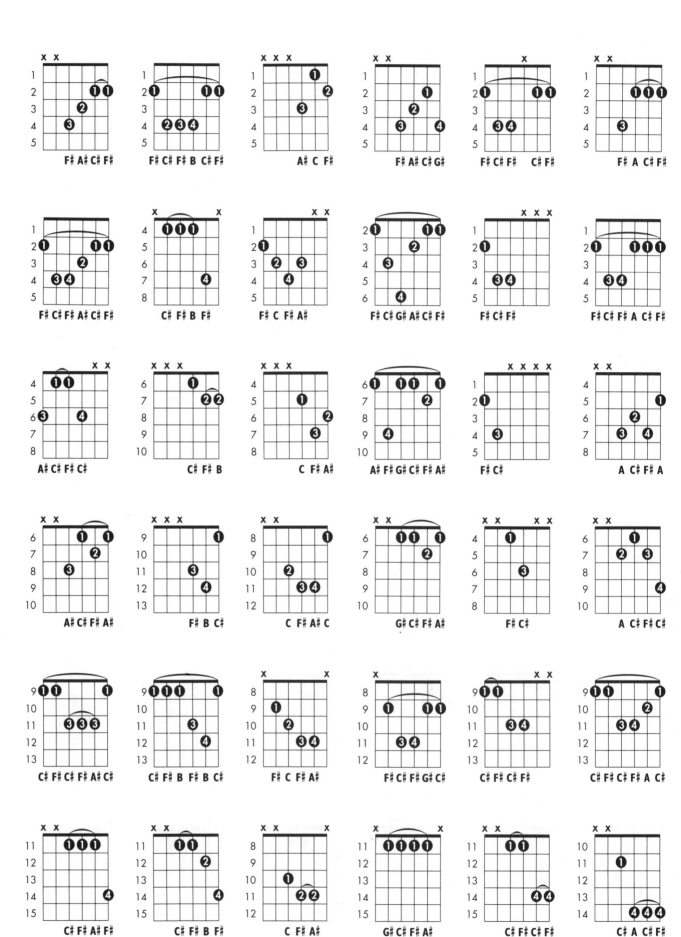

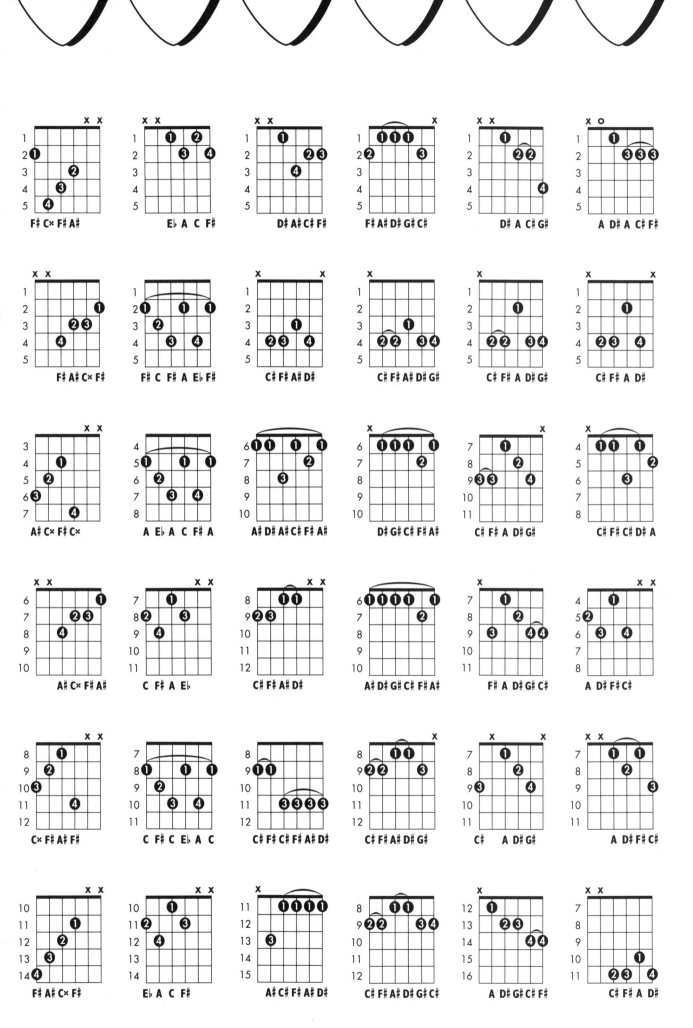

| F#7 | F#7sus | F#m7 | F#m7(♭5) | F#7+ | F#7(♭5) |
|-----|--------|------|----------|------|---------|

F# A# C# E | F# B C# E | F# C# E A | E A C F# | F# A# C× A# C× E | E A# C F#

F# C# E A# C# F# | F# C# E B C# F# | F# C# E A C# F# | F# C E A | E A# C× F# | F# C E A#

F# A# E F# | C# F# B E | F# C# E A | F# C E A | C× F# A# E | F# C E A#

C# F# A# E | B E F# C# | E A C# F# | E A C F# | E A# C× F# | A# E F# C

C# F# C# E A# C# | C# F# B E | C# F# C# E A C# | E A E F# C | C× F# A# E | C F# A# E

**F#**

C# F# A# E | C# F# B E | C# F# A E | F# C E A | C× F# A# E | C F# A# E

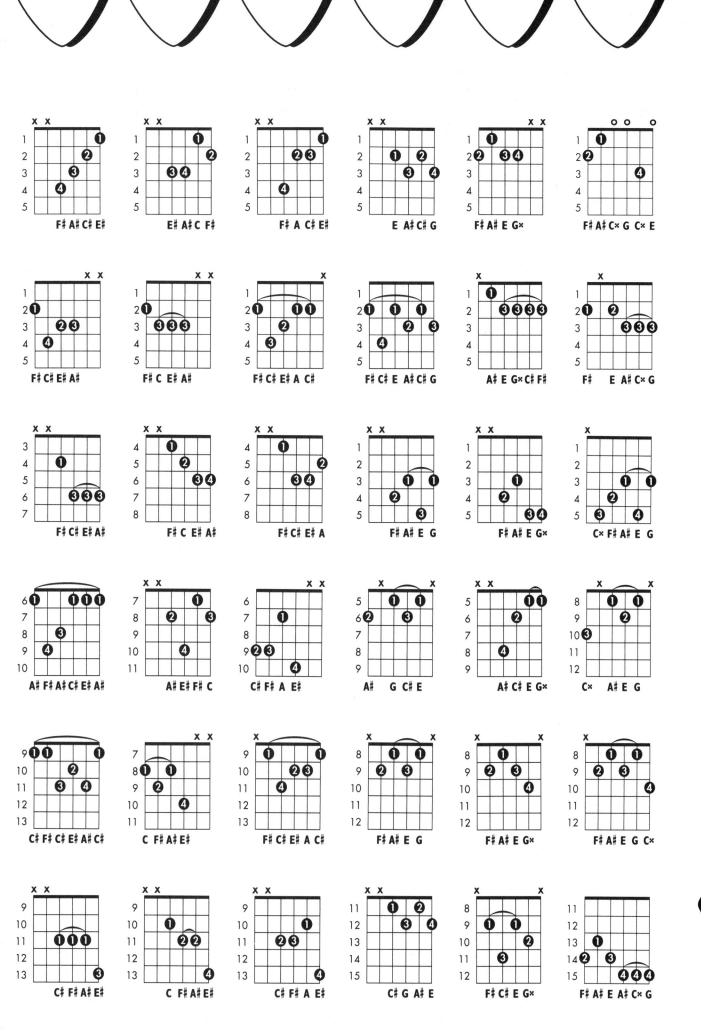

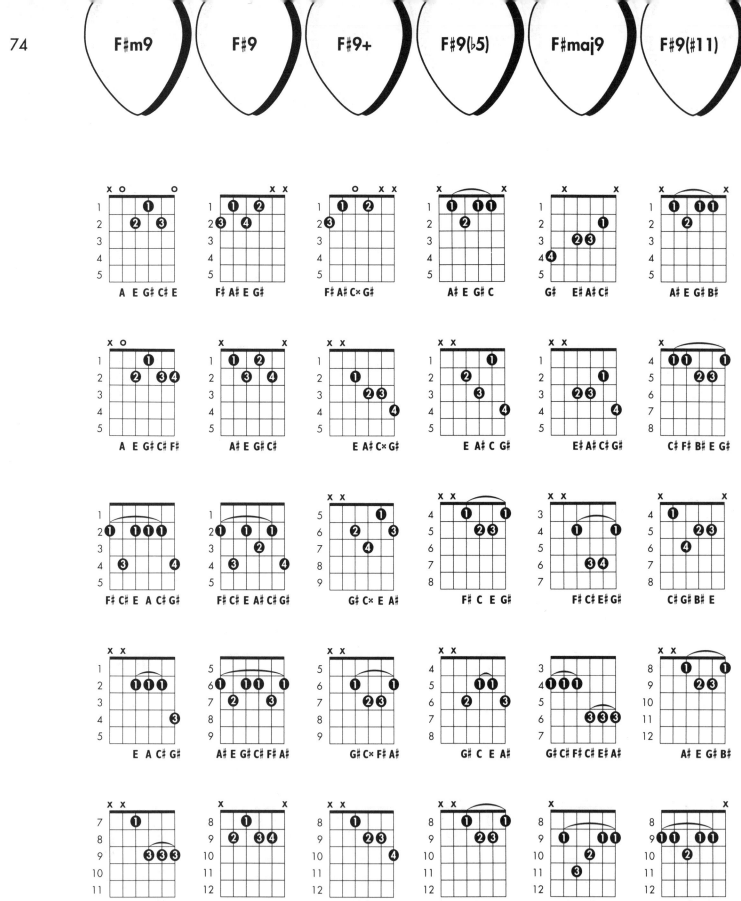

F#m9 · F#9 · F#9+ · F#9(♭5) · F#maj9 · F#9(#11)

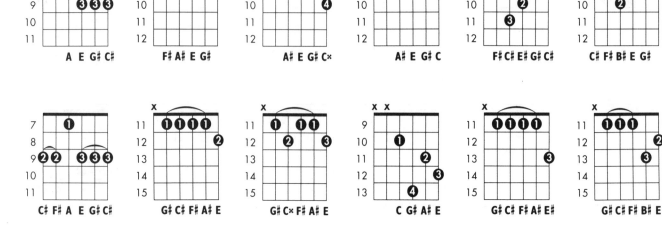

F#

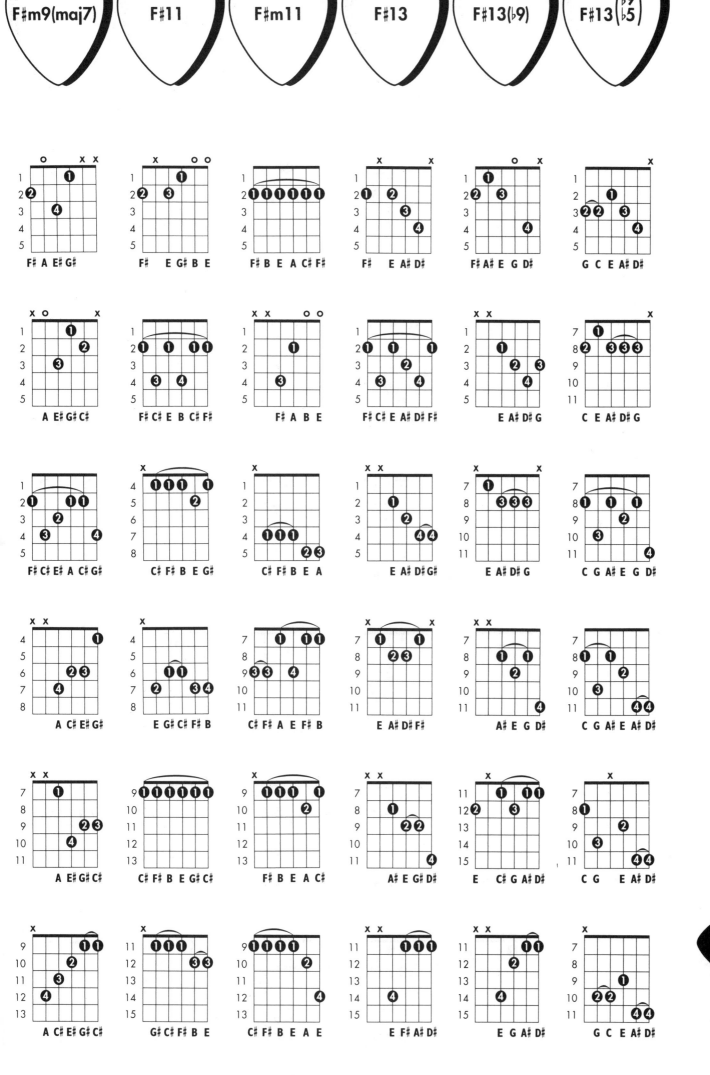

F#m9(maj7) · F#11 · F#m11 · F#13 · F#13(♭9) · F#13(♭9♭5)

F#

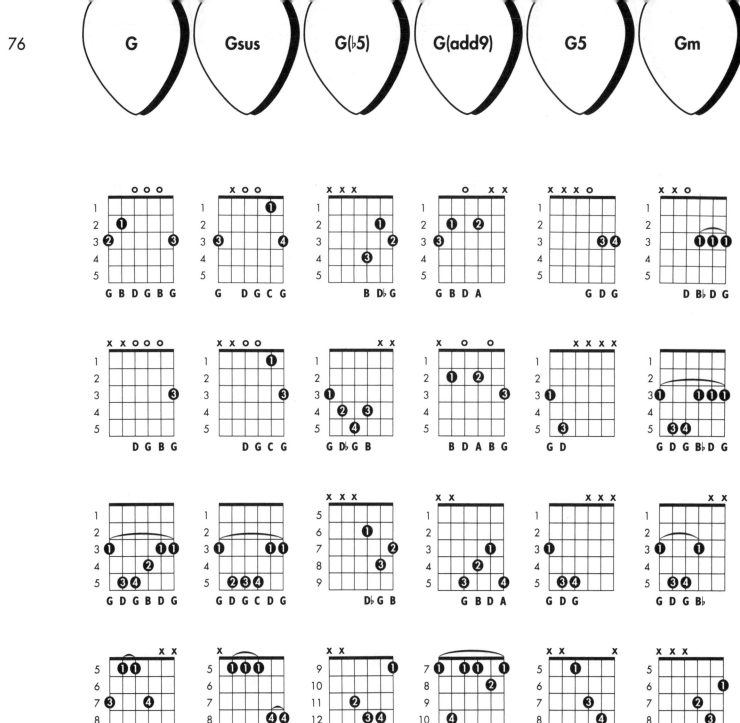

## G+    G°    G6    G6/9    Gm6/9    Gm6

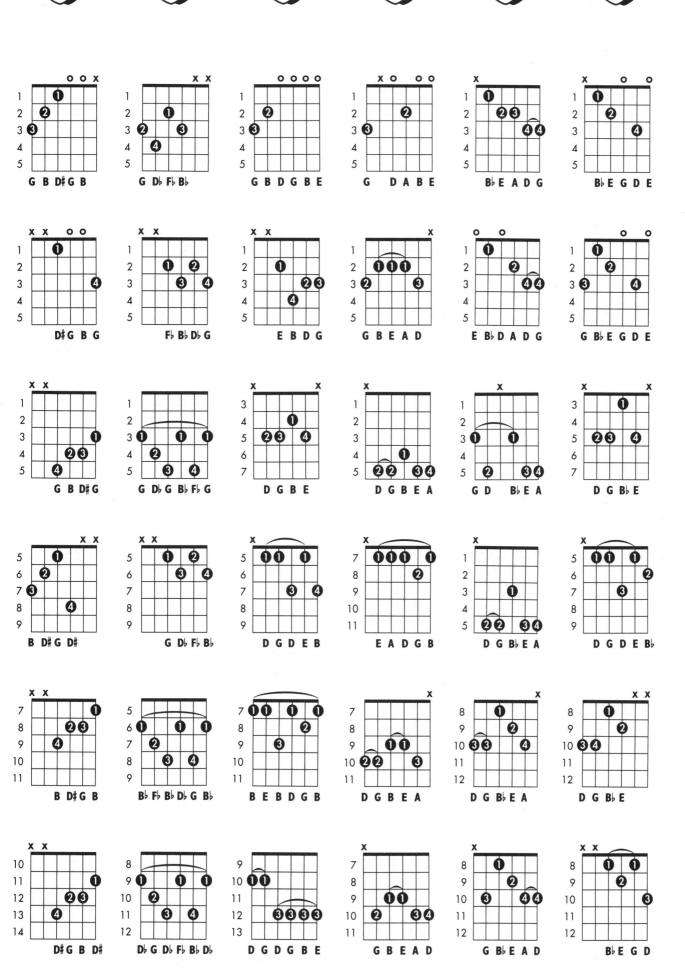

G+
G B D# G B

G°
G Db Fb Bb

G6
G B D G B E

G6/9
G D A B E

Gm6/9
Bb E A D G

Gm6
Bb E G D E

D# G B G

Fb Bb Db G

E B D G

G B E A D

E Bb D A D G

G Bb E G D E

G B D# G

G Db G Bb Fb G

D G B E

D G B E A

G D Bb E A

D G Bb E

B D# G D#

G Db Fb Bb

D G D E B

E A D G B

D G Bb E A

D G D E Bb

B D# G B

Bb Fb Bb Db G Bb

B E B D G B

D G B E A

D G Bb E A

D G Bb E

D# G B D#

Db G Db Fb Bb Db

D G D G B E

G B E A D

G Bb E A D

Bb E G D

G

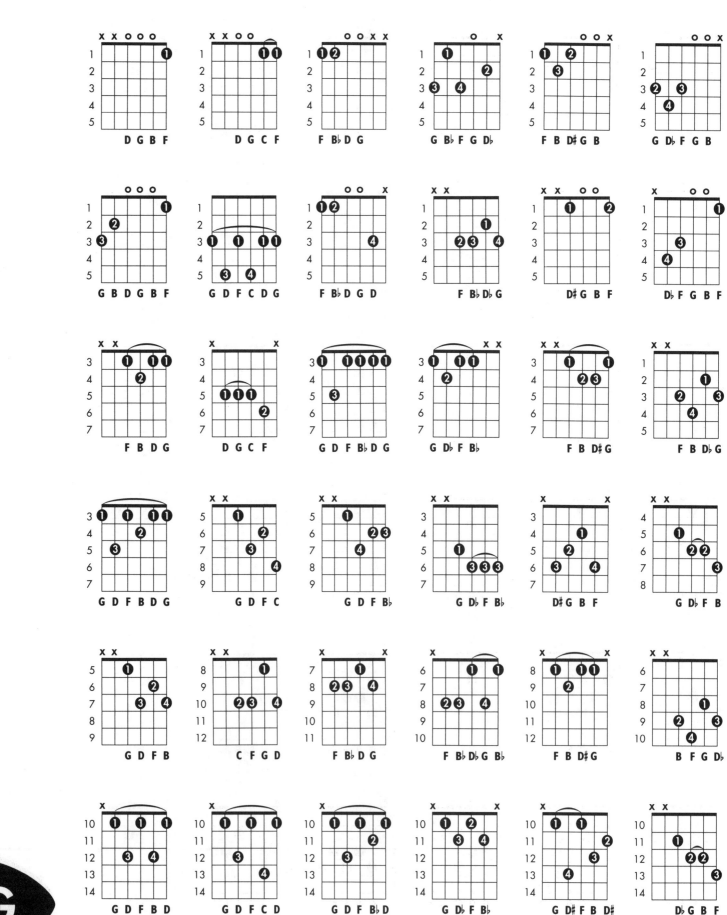

G

# Gmaj7   Gmaj7(♭5)   Gm(maj7)   G7(♭9)   G7(#9)   G7+(♭9)

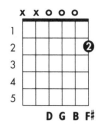 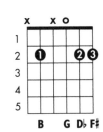 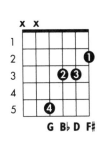 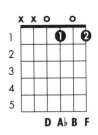  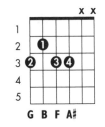

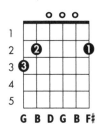 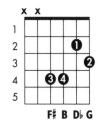 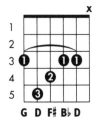 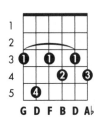 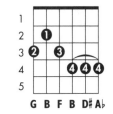 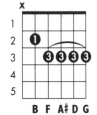

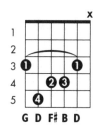 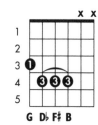 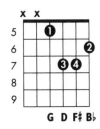 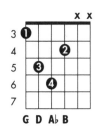 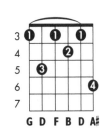 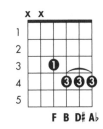

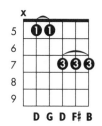 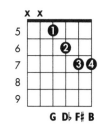 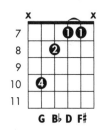 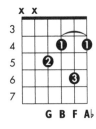 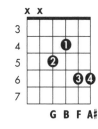 

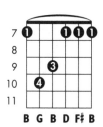 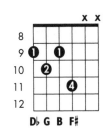 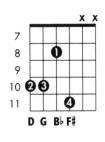 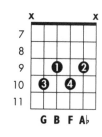 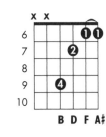 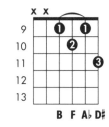

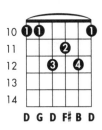 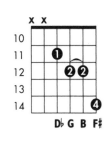 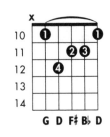 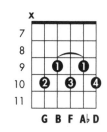 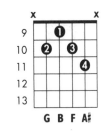 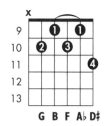

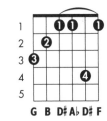

G

**Gm**    **G9**    **G9+**    **G9(♭5)**    **Gmaj9**    **G9(♯11)**

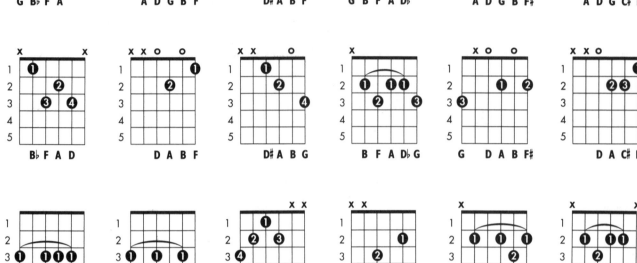

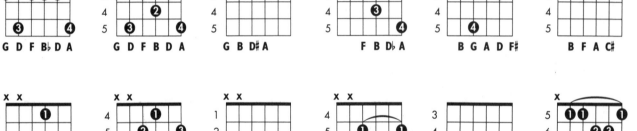

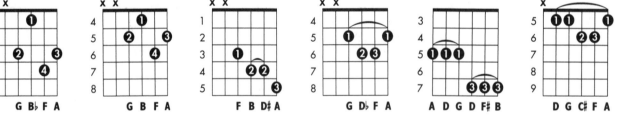

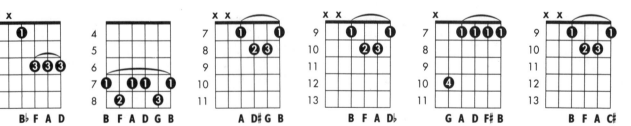

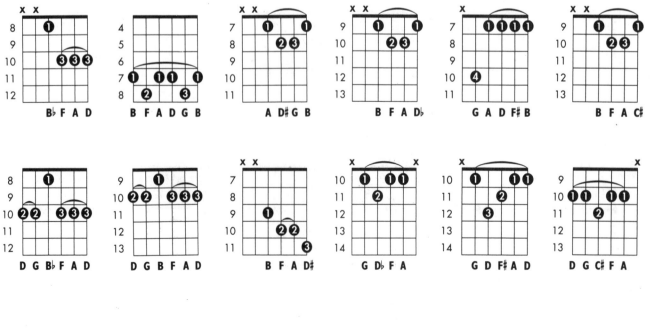

**G**